𝕿𝖍𝖊 𝕭𝖔𝖍𝖑𝖊𝖓

THE

EVIDENTIAL VALUE

OF THE

ACTS OF THE APOSTLES

BY THE

VERY REV. J S. HOWSON, D.D.

DEAN OF CHESTER, ENGLAND

DELIVERED IN THE CHURCH OF THE HOLY TRINITY, PHILA-
DELPHIA, IN APRIL, 1880

WIPF & STOCK · Eugene, Oregon

Wipf and Stock Publishers
199 W 8th Ave, Suite 3
Eugene, OR 97401

The Evidential Value of the Acts of the Apostles
The Bohlen Lectures 1880
By Howson, J. S.
Softcover ISBN-13: 978-1-6667-0493-8
Hardcover ISBN-13: 978-1-6667-0494-5
eBook ISBN-13: 978-1-6667-0495-2
Publication date 3/9/2021
Previously published by
E. P. Dutton and Company, 1880

THE JOHN BOHLEN LECTURESHIP.

JOHN BOHLEN, who died in this city on the 26th day of April, 1874, bequeathed to trustees a fund of One Hundred Thousand Dollars, to be distributed to religious and charitable objects in accordance with the well-known wishes of the testator.

By a deed of trust, executed June 2, 1875, the trustees under the will of Mr Bohlen transferred and paid over to "The Rector, Church Wardens, and Vestrymen of the Church of the Holy Trinity, Philadelphia," in trust, a sum of money for certain designated purposes, out of which fund the sum of Ten Thousand Dollars was set apart for the endowment of THE JOHN BOHLEN LECTURESHIP, upon the following terms and conditions —

The money shall be invested in good substantial and safe securities, and held in trust for a fund to be called The John Bohlen Lectureship, and the income shall be applied annually to the payment of a qualified person, whether clergyman or layman, for the delivery and publication of at least one hundred copies of two or more lecture sermons   These Lectures shall be delivered at such time and place, in the city of Philadelphia, as the persons nominated to appoint the lecturer shall from time to time determine, giving at least six months notice to the person appointed to deliver the same, when the same may conveniently be done, and in no case selecting the same person as lecturer a second time within a period of five years   The payment shall be made to said lecturer, after the lectures have been printed and received by the trustees, of all the income for the year derived from said fund, after defraying the expense of printing the lectures and the other incidental expenses attending the same

The subject of such lectures shall be such as is within the terms set forth in the will of the Rev. John Bampton, for the delivery of what are known as the "Bampton Lectures," at Oxford, or any other subject distinctively connected with or relating to the Christian Religion.

The lecturer shall be appointed annually in the month of May, or as soon thereafter as can conveniently be done, by the persons, who for the time being, shall hold the offices of Bishop of the Protestant Episcopal Church of the Diocese in which is the Church of the Holy Trinity, the Rector of said Church; the Professor of Biblical Learning, the Professor of Systematic Divinity, and the Professor of Ecclesiastical History, in the Divinity School of the Protestant Episcopal Church in Philadelphia

In case either of said offices are vacant the others may nominate the lecturer.

Under this trust the Very Rev. J S. Howson, D.D., Dean of Chester Cathedral, England, was appointed to deliver the lectures for the year 1880.

PHILADELPHIA, Easter-tide, 1880.

CONTENTS.

———•◇•———

LECTURE I.

LECTURE I.

GENERAL CHARACTERISTICS OF THE BOOK.

THE EVIDENTIAL VALUE OF THE ACTS OF THE APOSTLES.

LECTURE I.

GENERAL CHARACTERISTICS OF THE BOOK.

THE invitation which has brought me across the Ocean, to associate myself once more with religious thought in America, was very welcome when I received it. After a little hesitation, chiefly connected with a sense of my inadequacy for the task proposed to me, I gladly and thankfully consented to come. I am very conscious indeed that I cannot rival, either in depth or in breadth of thought, the three who have preceded me in this lectureship: and, instead of precisely following their steps, I think I shall take a wiser estimate of my own ability, and shall show a truer respect to my audience and the trustees, if I only attempt a superficial treatment of things familiar.

The ground of the Acts of the Apostles is

that part of the large and varied field of the Bible which my footsteps have most frequently trod. There are indications too of a sense in the Church at large that this book has hardly received all the attention it deserves. Chrysostom complained that in his day it was too much neglected. In our own day it would not be unreasonable if a similar complaint were made. Among the recent indications of an increasing interest in the book I class the commentaries of two authors of your own, Alexander and Hackett, one of whom I had the honor of knowing personally, while the other I have learnt to respect through some acquaintance with his writings. There are various circumstances, too, which appear to show that this book supplies teaching peculiarly useful in our present state of thought. Moreover it must, in the very nature of the case, be essentially bound up with the historical basis of Christianity. And it has been assailed in our time, if with some degree of perverseness, yet with great ingenuity; while, on the other hand, it has received new confirmatory illustrations of high value during the last fifty years. For all these reasons the book seems to press for itself a claim on our attention, which previously was not felt to be so urgent.

Thus I propose for our subject the evidential value, or, to state the same thing in a more German fashion, the apologetic worth of the Acts of the Apostles. I ask you to join me in examining this book, with the view of seeing how, in itself and in its relation to other things, it justifies its sacred position; how it comes to us with a divine recommendation on its face; how it stands a close scrutiny without being harmed, how it holds out its hands and amicably clasps, on the one side, the Gospel history, and on the other side the writings of the Apostles. These two relations of this book with contiguous parts of the New Testament, on either hand, will form the subjects of the second and third lectures. The fourth will deal with the practical benefit, as to instruction and edification, which is to be derived from this part of Holy Scripture The present introductory lecture may fitly have regard for the most part to some of its general characteristics, some of those features of the book, which win our confidence, simply as we look upon them.

The best way to estimate the value of a treasure is to inquire what our position would be if we ceased to possess it. A good question to ask ourselves, when we are reading some particular book of the Scriptures is this: What should we lose, and what would the Church lose, if this particular book of the Bible which I am reading were wanting? Suppose, for the sake of illustration, before we proceed further, that we apply this test to that earlier writing of St. Luke, the Gospel which bears his name. What would be our loss, if this third Gospel were to become a blank, if mankind had never seen it, or if mankind were absolutely to forget that it ever existed?

For a ready answer to this question, our thoughts rush at once to the special contents of this Gospel. But before giving this answer in detail, let us pause for a moment (it is not irrelevant to our subject) to see if

there is not another part of the answer which
our hearts suggest to us with a power quite
as great as any conviction that comes through
the intellect. There are two ways of study-
ing the biographies of our Lord and Saviour.
We may either combine them, so as to obtain a complete picture of the character and
influence and power of That Sacred Life: and
this is the common way in which the impression of Christ is made upon the world;
or we may separate the four evangelists, so
as to mark how they differ from one another:
and it is this kind of study and observation
to which the question just asked invites us.
But before we turn to that separate analysis,
are we not conscious of what we owe to St.
Luke, even if we are contemplating *the general
result* of the combined and complete picture?
In a great and successful portrait there are
many varied touches which make it what it
is, and which are essential to the expression
of the whole. Now in St. Luke there is a
certain tenderness of tone, a certain charm
of delicate coloring, a cheerful atmosphere, a

bright encouragement, a human light, as it were, on those Divine Features, without which the picture would not be what it is. It would be easy to analyze this and to explain it, if this were our point for the moment; and I just name, in explanation, two special characteristics of this Gospel by the way. These are the sympathetic mention of widows and the honorable mention of Samaritans in this book. My wish, however, at this point is to invite attention to the fact that we cannot rightly estimate the value of St Luke's Gospel without considering how his work blends with the other three. If we had these three alone the world would not simply be the poorer, but it would be liable to that kind of error which arises from lack of completeness. Thus much may fairly be said, evidentially, on the general impression derived from St. Luke's Gospel, irrespective of its special contents.

And now, if we are to give the answer which is derived from a consideration of the contents of this Gospel, we are at no loss, and a very few words will suffice. It is

not possible here to do more than to select some specimens. In St. Luke, at the
beginning, we have those hymns of the New
Testament, connected with the Nativity of our
Lord, which make every English Christmas
joyous; and an English Christmas is part of
the inheritance of America. In St. Luke, at
the end, we have the story of that journey to
Emmaus, which Cowper, perhaps less frequently read now, both in America and in England,
than he ought to be, has brought, in his
charming manner, into most practical connection with our home-life. From St. Luke
only have we those encouragements to prayer,
which are supplied in the Parables of the
Midnight Traveller and the Unjust Judge.
In St Luke only have we the lessons of deep
humility, and of mercy to the penitent, in the
Parables of the Pharisee and Publican and of
the Prodigal Son. Luke only tells us of the
welcome given to the converted malefactor,
who was crucified by the side of Christ. This
is the Gospel of large toleration, of tender sympathy, of cheerful hope, of joyous thanksgiv-

ing. Good reason indeed we have, throughout the ages, to be grateful to him, who
under God, from his own point of view,
wrote these things "in order" to the "most
excellent Theophilus," that we too in distant
lands, might know "the certainty of those
things, in which we have been instructed."

And if from "the former treatise" we turn
to the second and ask ourselves — following
the same method of thought—what is the
special value to us of the Acts of the Apostles, — if we ask ourselves, what we should
lose, and what our Christianity would lose,
supposing this book to be obliterated from
our Bibles, the mere proposing of the question makes us almost start at the contemplation of the magnitude of the treasure which
we here possess. I have spoken above of its
connection with the Gospels on one side and
with the Epistles on the other. What if this
book were not here? What a chasm would
then yawn, to bewilder and alarm us, between these two very diverse parts of the
New Testament! The Gospels on the one

side, and the Epistles on the other, and nothing between—what a vacant space to be peopled with all manner of fancies and apparitions! what a difficulty for even discreet minds to establish the true connection between the writings of St. Paul and the records of the Evangelists! Even with this solid connection established, and with all the sober coloring which rests upon it, we have seen what wild speculation can do to build up theories and to suggest inconsistencies But, having this book for a perpetual possession, the Church has all that it really needs, as regards this subject, if not for full satisfaction, yet for full benefit. The mere fact that the want is supplied, that we possess this treasure, seems to me a proof that it is Divinely given. "Every good and perfect gift comes from above, from the Father of lights, with whom is no variableness, neither shadow of turning." Though I am writing evidentially, I am addressing Christians; and from them this argument will meet an immediate response.

And what if the contents, the arrangement,

the limitations, of this book are somewhat different from what we should *à priori* have expected? This is our state of mind in regard to the whole of the Bible. And indeed of all God's gifts it is true that they are different from what we might have anticipated. We might perhaps, following our impulsive reasoning, have looked in this great intermediate treatise for something more systematic in the definitions of Doctrine and in rules of Discipline, and considerably less in the form of mere personal incident. As regards its remarkably biographical character, this it has in common with the rest of the Bible; and so far there is an argument in its favor derived from consistency. But, speaking generally, there are, it is true, many things in the Acts of the Apostles different from what we should have anticipated. For instance, we might wish that we had a symmetrical account of each of the twelve Apostles, after the manner of the fabled origin of the sentences of the Apostles' Creed. We may be disappointed that we learn nothing of that diffused work of St. Peter,

which produced in the East effects co-ordinate
with and correlative to the results of St. Paul's
preaching in the West. And when, leaving
the former Apostle behind, we encounter in
this book the great personality of St Paul,
we may wonder why so large a space is given
to a voyage and a shipwreck, where the very
name of God is but scantily mentioned, while
we long in vain for full details of his missionary and pastoral work during the eigh-
teen months at Corinth or the three years at
Ephesus. But it does not follow, because
there are some things in the gift which surprise us, that therefore the gift is not good.
The supreme wisdom of the Giver is, to the
devout mind, the measure of its thankfulness.

Again, let us mark this important feature
of the case, that the book before us is *quite
unique.* If we were to lose it from the Bible,
there is no book else that could stand in its
place There is none other at all like it, or
that covers any part of the same ground. If
one of the four Gospels were lost, we should
have still three Gospels remaining, and a

CHRIST, familiar and dear to us, whom we could reverence and adore. If even two or three Apostolic Epistles were to vanish, still more than a dozen such documents would remain in our hands, to tell us what Christianity is, and to insist upon its claims. But if the Book of Acts were gone, there would be nothing to replace it : and we may go further and say that the Christian Scriptures would then lie before us in two disjointed fragments. The complete arch would not be built. In a very true sense it may be asserted that the Book of the Acts is the keystone of this part of the Bible. The very perfection thus given to the structure seems to show that the structure itself is not accidental The Divine gift of the New Testament appears to us all the more Divine, because the Acts of the Apostles make it complete in all its parts.

Negatively then, even in regard to our instinctive consciousness of its value, this Book of the Acts comes to us with high claims on our confident welcome and grateful allegiance. And we can adopt moreover another negative mode of putting an estimate on its worth. There are certain Apocryphal Acts of the Apostles, not very much known to the Christian world at large, but yet copious and varied, which we can place side by side with the Canonical Acts; and we are in some degree able to appreciate the worth of the former by comparison with the latter. This Apocryphal literature of the second and third centuries has been recently brought to view more than formerly; and the most has been made of it by those who are disposed to make the least of our Authentic Scriptures Leaving all the rest of this literature aside, I will just name three of the documents which it contains, the "Acts of Paul and Thecla," the "Clementine Homilies," of which the hero is Peter, and thirdly, the "Acts of Peter and Paul," with the view of pointing out what kind of impression our familiar and venerable history of these two Apostles makes on our minds, in comparison with those other Acts.

The scene of "the Acts of Paul and Thecla," is laid chiefly at Iconium. Names of places

and persons suggested by the New Testament,
such as Daphne, Lystra, and Myra on the one
hand, and Onesiphorus, Tryphæna, and Demas
on the other, seem to be put together in this
document very much at random. Even its
geography forms a strong contrast with the
geography of St. Luke's history. No very
clear distinction is drawn between the Pisid-
ian Antioch and the Syrian Antioch, and
Lystra is put in its wrong place as regards
the former city. But especially must be noted
its utter want of dignity, as constituting a
strong contrast with the Evangelist's elevat-
ing narrative. Two of the chief features of
this Apocryphal work are a fantastic love-
story, and a form of asceticism quite different
from what is inculcated in the New Testament
And let it not be said that it is waste of time
to make mention of a document now obsolete
and forgotten Once these Acts of Paul and
Thecla were publicly read in church What
if they had now been recognized as part of
the New Testament? We can appreciate the
value of such an escape, when we think what

it would have been, if we were compelled to view the story of Bel and the Dragon as part of the Old.

A much larger space in literature is filled by what we know as the "Clementines." We are acquainted with them in two forms—the "Homilies," of which the Greek text is extant, and the "Recognitions," of which we possess only a Latin translation. The theory on which they are based is not simply that there was a long continued antagonism between the disciples of St. Peter and the disciples of St. Paul, but that there was a sharp antagonism between those Apostles themselves—a theory which has now been actively revived; and the general drift of this production is to glorify the former at the expense of the latter   It may suffice here to quote Baron de Bunsen, who was by no means restricted and narrow in his orthodoxy   He regards these Acts of Peter as a pure fiction, and protests against the modern attempt of Baur to supplant history by means of a novel. This subject of the Pseudo-Clementines must be referred to hereafter   All

that need be said on the general subject here
is that because there were antagonistic parties
afterwards appealing to the names of Peter
and Paul, it does not follow that those two
Apostles were opposed We see their unity
in the Acts of the Apostles If on the as-
sumption of their antagonism it is concluded
that the Acts of the Apostles were written
to produce an imaginary reconcilement of such
antagonism — by this kind of reasoning any
theory in the world might be constructed
The best answer to such fancies is to note the
transparent truthfulness and noble tone of the
Acts of the Apostles, their direct singleness
of purpose, and the absence from them of
all dreamy speculative discussion ; and these
are the features of the book on which I am
now laying stress. Judging by mere impression it is easy to say confidently—on a comparison of the two documents—that the Acts
represent reality and that the Pseudo-Clementines are a romance.

A third Apocryphal document, which is not
altogether destitute of dignity and beauty, is

entitled the "Acts of Peter and Paul" That
this document is a random composition is
evident from its geographical inaccuracy. In
the authentic account of St Paul's voyage
from Malta to Puteoli, it is distinctly said
that the ship staid one day at Rhegium, and
this statement is expressly connected with a
change of wind, which admitted of no delay;
and it is added that they arrived at Puteoli
the "next day"; whereas in these Apocryphal Acts it is stated that Paul went across
from Rhegium to Messina, and there ordained
a bishop We see here most distinctly the
traces of a later period. On the other hand
we have in this document the most express
recognition of the unity of Peter and Paul in
their spirit and their teaching. Thus one set
of Apocryphal Acts may be used as a counter-
poise to others

On the whole there is no reason to regret
that great pains have lately been taken to
bring all literature of this class more fully to
view than of old The more, it seems to me,
that such Apocryphal Acts are read, the bet-

ter. The more carefully such writings are
placed all around the Scriptural narrative
and compared with it, the more does that
narrative tower above them all, like a moun-
tain above lower hazy heights, with a golden
light ever upon its summit.

Thus far the argument for the value of the
Acts of the Apostles has been negative. In
the remainder of our time we must look at its
positive side And here I am disposed, in
the first place, to lay great stress on broad
and general characteristics. What an honest,
healthy tone there is in the book ! Its spirit
is altogether wholesome throughout It is
like the fresh breezy air of the mountains
or the sea There is nothing morbid in it
from beginning to end. No one can study it
without being made better How bright too
and encouraging are these early annals of
Apostolic adventure and success ! How like
they are, in this respect, to the Gospel of
St. Luke ! The book has been termed an
Evangelical Odyssey We can hardly accept
this description as altogether correct for the

book throughout is intensely serious and solemn: but we ought not to overlook that
freshness and cheerfulness which suggested
the description

And in order to give definiteness to an impression of which we all must be conscious, I
am inclined to fix on two characteristics of
the book, first its transparent truthfulness,
secondly the noble generosity of its tone.

As to its *truthfulness*, I think we might easily test this without any minute criticism. And
this, in some respects, is better than any other test. How artless is the narrative! While
minute and full of detail, how simple is the
telling of the story, how remote from any show
of contrivance; how free from any nervous anx-
iety to justify or excuse itself, or to prove its
own consistency! For instance, how honestly
are recorded the inconsistencies of the early
Church and the faults of some of its leading
men. The mean selfishness of Ananias and
Sapphira are related at the very fore-front.
The historian is not ashamed to say that the
first organization of a Christian ministry arose

out of a dispute among some widows. Again,
it is not concealed that the wider diffusion
of missionary work was developed in consequence of a quarrel between Barnabas and Paul
through the defection of Mark. So again at
Ephesus, Luke chronicles the shame as well as
the glory of the Church, and tells us that some
of its members, while joining in its sacred rites,
associated themselves also with the occult arts
of necromancy As regards the great Apostle
himself, his hasty angry answer to the high
priest is recorded with as much straightforward simplicity as his speech to the Lystrians
and his defence before Festus. And to turn
to another aspect of truthfulness, how admirable are some of the descriptions, as for instance
in the accounts of the mobs at Ephesus and
Jerusalem ! What an air of reality pervades
these two stories ! In the sagacious appeasing
of the tumult by the town-clerk in the former
instance, and in the adroitness with which the
Apostle, after speaking in Greek to the Roman officer, turns round to address the angry crowd in Hebrew,—in both these cases

we might almost say that there is a touch of humor Or to take two other parallel scenes of a totally different kind. Twice St Paul is described as among untutored heathens, who spoke some language which was neither Greek nor Latin· and in each case the story is singularly true to nature On one occasion, after the working of a miracle, there is an attempt to worship him as a god, and then under the influence of fanatical Jews he is stoned. On the other occasion, because a viper fastens upon his hand, he is believed to be a murderer, and then because the viper does not hurt him, he is believed to be a god How thoroughly natural too are the touches of character which we find in various parts of the book ! Take, for instance, the manifest falsehood introduced into the letter of Claudius Lysias, when he finds that he has been trifling with St. Paul's Roman citizenship, or the equally manifest falsehood in the speech of Tertullus, when he is retained as counsel by the Jews, to secure, if possible, St Paul's condemnation. And, to give just one more example, how thoroughly like what we should expect from a Roman official, in the presence of angry fanatics and of religious questions which he does not understand, is the conduct of Gallio at Corinth! Nothing is said here of the correspondence of his conduct with the character which is given of him in history. That subject will properly belong to the last lecture I am speaking here of what is true to nature, not of what is true to historic fact. All that is pointed out here, is the honesty of the Acts of the Apostles, as gathered from what we see on the very surface of its narration And I will just add this remark, that a general impression of this kind, ranging over a great number and variety of incidents, is of a high value

Here, however, we are partly engaged in an evidential inquiry and it is desirable for a few moments to look below the surface Moreover an instinctive impression of natural truthfulness ought to stand the test of criticisms An impression of this kind can be submitted to cross-examination. We feel a narrative to be naturally and truthfully told; and we ask ourselves what are the marks by which we can examine and justify such an impression. I will invite you then to join me, while I apply this method of close criticism to one selected passage of the Acts of the Apostles

There are two accounts of the conversion of Cornelius; one given by St Luke in the direct narrative of the tenth chapter; the other by St Peter, when defending himself before the apostles and elders at Jerusalem, as recorded in the eleventh. I suppose the general impression of most readers, as to this reiteration, would be this, that, the occasion being very important, it is intentionally made emphatic in this way And to this view I should see no objection, *if we had simply* a case of reiteration before us. The Bishop of Lincoln devoutly says here that the Holy Spirit, in the structure of Scripture, does not disdain to use repetition: Reuss says that we have here a specimen of the Oriental style of narration, and neither of these opinions need be

blamed, nor are they inconsistent with one
another. But, as I have implied, we have in
this place not to deal with a case of mere reiteration. On the second occasion, when the
conversion of Cornelius is related, St. Peter is
speaking under apologetic conditions. He addresses himself therefore to the emergency, as
any sensible man would do, speaking at such
a moment under a serious sense of responsi-
bility. The expostulation was—" Thou went-
est in to men uncircumcised, and didst eat with
them " His task (and it was a difficult one)
was to convince those who, under deep-rooted
prejudice, so expostulated. Hence he omits
certain things which appear in St Luke's narrative, but which are of no moment to his
argument Certain points again in that narrative he repeats with care, and lays special
stress upon them. Certain other things he
adds; and we should not have known them
at all, were it not that St. Peter was called
upon thus to justify and defend himself before
his fellow-apostles and others. Let us look
at his speech under these three heads.

He does not say that when the vision came
to him he was on the housetop, or that it was
midday, or that he was hungry, or that they
were preparing his meal when the sheet de-
scended, or that he "came down" from the
roof to meet the messengers   All these things,
though most interesting in the narrative, and
indeed important for the natural telling of
the story, were of no argumentative value in
the serious effort of the moment. Again, he
does not say any thing about that animated
part of the story, in which the messengers are
described as inquiring their way to "the house
of Simon the tanner." All such particulars
were outside his own experience; and it would
have been unreal, perhaps suspicious, to have
named them.   But, again, he does not say that
Cornelius was a centurion. He calls him simply "the man" at Cæsarea   The fact that he
was a Roman soldier would not predispose any
Jew to regard him with complacency. Nor
does Peter describe the admirable character
of Cornelius, which is made so prominent in
the direct narrative   For the exercise of moral

persuasion upon him at Joppa, in reference to the extraordinary summons he was receiving to go to Cæsarea, this description was of high importance One of the lessons he was to learn was that God's distinctions between one man and another rest on moral grounds, and that it is possible for a heathen to be drawn by the grace of God towards the highest good without any Judaism intervening But such a view presented abruptly to "the apostles and elders" at that moment might have created a prejudice in their minds, and made them reluctant to listen They were not disposed as yet to think that any high virtues could exist, irrespective of Judaic conditions.

But on certain things named by the direct historian St. Peter does lay special stress, knowing that they will tell upon the conviction of his hearers Thus he says that he was *praying*, when the vision came Whatever lingering prejudice there might have been in the minds of the Apostles, they knew what their Lord had said concerning prayer and the answer to prayer. Again Peter noted strongly

the remarkable coincidence as to time and circumstance, in this wonderful experience; and
they had the fullest belief (and they would
have had the fullest belief, even if they had
not heard the Sermon on the Mount) in the
minute guiding of Special Providence. Again,
he laid emphatic stress on that voice of the
Holy Ghost, which since the day of Pentecost,
in fulfilment of the promise, had become to
them an articulate voice. Once more, though
he does not disturb the minds of his hearers
by speaking of the character of Cornelius, he
does tell them expressly that "an angel" had
appeared to him   This fact brought the occurrences in his house within the range of those
recognized Divine communications, of which
they had had familiar instances in the history
of the Old Testament   And still once again,
though he does not give unimportant details
of place and person (does not say, for instance,
that he was lodging "in the house of Simon
the tanner") he does specify most strongly
the personal form of the message which came
from Cæsarea   "*Simon, which is surnamed*

Peter"—four times in this whole narrative of the Conversion of Cornelius does this significant phrase occur They well knew that the Lord had given to him this surname. The reiteration too (for here is reiteration) made the surname very definite to their minds, as it had been made to his. Moreover it expressed his strong personal conviction that he had received a call to a special mission, so that, to quote words used by himself long afterwards, the Gentiles "*by his mouth*" were first to hear directly of Christ All these things touched them very closely, and must have gathered gradually into an irresistible argument.

And now, in the third place, let me point out certain things which Peter, while telling his own story, added to the circumstances related by St. Luke. He says that the voice came to him "from heaven " He says that the sheet gradually approached to him and came near to him. He says that he looked upon its contents intently and gazed deliberately. All this is part of the natural vividness

with which a man gives the account of what
has happened to himself But moreover it
tended to show to his hearers that the teaching which came to him through this vision,
was no mere vague impression, but a very de-
liberate conviction, seriously accepted. And
finally mark how he calls attention to the
witnesses and the companions of his journey to Cæsarea. "Moreover *these six brethren* accompanied me" But for this pointed
and lively reference in his speech we should
not have known that there were "six." Nor
should we have known from what is related
in the direct narrative that he took these six
men with him *to Jerusalem* (in itself a most
important and convincing fact) to attest the
truth of this great transaction. Above all,
when he comes to speak of the descent of the
Holy Ghost at Cæsarea, he describes the pro-
cess of his own mind. "Then remembered I
the word of the Lord." They too had heard
the same word of the Lord. I shall have occasion to refer to this point again in the next
lecture, as an illustration of the connection

between the Acts and the Gospels. Here I
adduce it only as an indication of natural
truthfulness

This analysis of the relation between the
tenth and eleventh chapters of the Acts of
the Apostles is not by any means exhaustive.
It might be pursued even more minutely and
might be made more complete. But enough
has been said for my present purpose; and I
think it will be admitted that we have here
not by any means a case of mere bald reiteration, but on the contrary a most real and
artless specimen of the re-telling of a story
with such variations of emphasis and information as exactly fit the occasion. And will any
one say that all these minute differences and
correspondences were ingeniously invented, in
order, on examination, to produce the impression of an early and contemporary date in a
document really composed and put together
long afterwards ? In answer to *this* question
I will only make two remarks. I will ask you
first what your own impression would be on the
appearance of such phenomena in an examina-

tion of documents in a court of justice   And next I will take the liberty of adding, that, though I have a moderately good acquaintance with commentaries on the Acts of the Apostles, I never saw this argument definitely laid hold of, until I thought of it independently myself. Seventeen centuries is a long time to wait for the ingenuity of a forger in Alexandria or in Rome to find its reward here in Philadelphia.

I pass now to the other point—from the truthfulness which wins our confidence to the *generosity* which moves our hearts. Truthfulness and generosity—the two qualities are very nearly allied, whether in the individual character or in the religious tone of a book. If we see them then in conjunction here, each strengthens the evidence supplied by the other   There is presented to us all through the Acts of the Apostles a high, noble, and unselfish standard of Christian living. A generous self-effacement is the feature of those whom we see there acting as the chief characters. And this in itself is a Divine mark on the book which Christian hearts at least will readily recognize.

There is first the instinct and the habit of large and liberal giving for the relief of the poor and the distressed. I use the words "instinct" and "habit," because we see this feature of the Christian life both at the beginning and the end of the book. No sooner is the excitement of Pentecost over, than this sympathy and this spirit of mutual help show themselves in lavish giving We may say, if we will, that in the first method of practically manifesting this feeling there was a kind of communism, which it would not have been wise to continue. But even at this early stage of the history there appears no sentimental weakness. The terrible rebukes given to Ananias and Sapphira and to Simon Magus, must not be overlooked. Such indignation is the dark background, which is necessary in order to present true benevolence in its proper bright relief. We must mark too the pains and trouble that were taken afterwards in distributing the gifts of charity and in choosing

suitable agents. The road between Antioch
and Jerusalem was trod and re-trod by the
footsteps of those who conveyed these gifts.
And now, if we follow the course of St.
Paul's life, we find him working with his
own hands, both at Corinth and Ephesus,
and saying that he did this, that he might
furnish an example of helping others through
our own self-denial. At the latter of these
cities we mark how the inconsistent disciples, named above, who had tampered with
sorcery, manifested, when touched in conscience, their true Christian repentance by
giving up their "fifty thousand pieces of silver", and we can read between the lines and
see the indignation of St. Paul and St. Luke
against the sordid selfishness of Demetrius
and his craftsmen, who opposed Christianity,
because it was likely to undermine their prof-
its Above all we hear the Apostle quoting
that saying of Christ: "It is more blessed to
give than to receive,"—that golden proverb,
of which we should have known nothing,
were it not for the Acts of the Apostles.

And finally we find him saying, at the close of his last missionary journey, that he had come to Jerusalem "to bring alms to his nation," an intimation which, as we shall see, is an invaluable link with the Epistles Here I adduce it simply in illustration of a general characteristic of the Acts

It is the enumeration of such instances which justifies and explains our general impression of the tone of the book. And before I quit this topic I am tempted to go back to an earlier portion of the Acts, and to refer particularly to the scene in the house of Tabitha For my own part I am inclined to think that "the widows," both here and in the account of the institution of the deacons, were widows enrolled, not for the receiving of relief, but for the administration of relief. It is remarkable that the first organization of the deacons, the earliest-named part of the establishment of a Christian ministry, arose out of questions connected with practical charity It is to be noted also that the first mention of the presbyters occurs in connection with this very subject. If the suggestion I have ventured to make is a sound ·one, we reach a further point on the same line of thought; and we see ·that the very earliest ministry in the Church of Christ, under the Apostles, was a ministry of women for the exercise of sympathetic help

But not only generosity and charity, in respect of money and the relief of want, are characteristics of this document; but generosity and charity in the widest sense The spirit of self-effacement is conspicuous throughout. How readily the Apostles seem to stand aside, that they may give place to Stephen and even to Philip! But let us fix this portion of the Acts in our minds by reverting specially to the example of *Barnabas*. The Bible is so biographical in its structure, that in adopting this course, we are acting in true harmony with its spirit. Not only is Barnabas the great earliest example of lavish giving in the Church, and the great and bright contrast to the grudging meanness of Ananias and Sapphira; not

only is it to his hand that the alms of others
are afterward confided to convey and distrib-
ute; but he it is who introduces Paul to the
Apostles at one of the most critical moments
of his life; he it is who trusts, when all others
are distrustful, and removes a prejudice, which
otherwise would have hindered and clogged,
at its very outset, the career of the Apostle
of the Gentiles. He it is who, when tidings
came of the extraordinary success of the Gospel among the heathen at Antioch, was "sent
forth" that he might go thither. Why was he
elected ? I imagine it was because he was felt
to be the man most fitted for the enterprise by
large-heartedness and generosity of character.
He it is, who, "when he came to Antioch and
had seen the grace of God, was glad"· and it is
added: *"for he was a good man."* Why is this
added as a reason for what precedes ? The
word "good" here does not mean merely that
he was a man of earnest religious character.
This we know from the general context; nor
would this help us to the meaning of the connecting particle. The reason is given, why he

unfeignedly rejoiced in what he saw at Antioch There may have been misgivings and
suspicions at Jerusalem. but in his generous
heart there were none At this point of the
history we reach the climax of this charming
example He departed to Tarsus to seek the
newly-converted Paul ; at that time in obscurity, and "when he found him he brought
him to Antioch " He brought to that place
of active thought and active work, one whose
career was sure to supersede and eclipse his
own. Renan, with all his strange inconsistencies and wild theories, sometimes displays
extraordinary sagacity in seizing the true import of salient points in the apostolic history :
and his remarks concerning Barnabas are very
acute and happy. He says that "Christianity
has been unfair towards this great man in not
placing "him in the first rank among its found-
ers," that "every just and generous thought
had Barnabas for its patron " As to the particular point before us, the bringing of Saul
to Antioch, Renan says: " To gain *this mighty
soul,* to make himself its inferior, to prepare the

field most favorable for the development of its activity, while forgetting himself, this is surely the highest point which virtue ever reached The credit of St. Paul's career is due to the modest man, who put him forward on all occasions, obliterated himself in his presence, discovered what he was worth, placed him in the light, perceived beforehand the irremediable mischief which contemptible personalities might do to the work of God " I do not adopt Renan's words precisely, but they contain not a little truth Well may St Luke feel evident delight in describing such a character as that of Barnabas, and the Divine mark is on this part of the Acts of the Apostles, not only because of the noble standard it sets before us, but because it gives us an example capable of commonplace imitation

Even thus the instances are not exhausted which give to this Book of the Acts such an impress of noble generosity Some of the heathen, who are prominently mentioned there, themselves set this bright and cheerful example. Cornelius "gave much alms to the

Jewish people". the Asiarchs at Ephesus be-
friended St Paul · Julius "treated his prisoner
courteously" and allowed him to go on shore
for refreshment among his friends. The un-
lettered people in Malta "shewed no little
kindness" to the shipwrecked crew and passengers, both on their first reaching the shore,
and on their leaving the island three months
afterwards Publius too, "the chief man of
the island" manifested the same spirit These
are touches in the picture, singularly in harmony with the spirit of St Luke's Gospel, and
they ought not to be overlooked Of course
the feeling of charity *within the Christian
brotherhood* is and ought to be more intense,
and from this warm centre it radiates most
effectually outwards. This thought of brotherhood comes naturally into my mind as I
conclude. The name of this great city, in
which I am now permitted to lecture, ought,
I think, to be accepted as an encouraging
omen for the future of this world *Philadelphia*—in the deepest spiritual sense—*esto
perpetua* However separated we may be by

intervals of space, and by differences of occupation, however much we may be tried by
those who seek to divide us in things secu-
lar and things sacred, "let brotherly love
continue"

LECTURE II.

THE RELATION OF THIS BOOK TO THE GOSPEL HISTORY.

LECTURE II.

IN accordance with the plan briefly laid down in the last lecture, our occupation now is to consider this Book of the Acts in its connection with the Gospels, and to consider the subject in such a way as to keep in view any evidential results which appear as arising from this connection.

The point of meeting of St Luke's First and Second Treatises is *the Ascension of Christ* Let us mark this fact There is a wonderful fitness in this arrangement of the Bible Nothing could be more beautiful—nothing more full of meaning—nothing in more obvious harmony with the appointed transition from what Christ did on earth, to what He now does from heaven. We approach our subject by going up to the

Mount of Olives: and we gaze from thence back
upon the Gospel-time   To my mind there is
an 'evidential value in the very poetry of this
scene of the Ascension   Of course such a
thought cannot be pressed very far.   But let
us pause upon it for a moment   It is edify-
ing and consoling.   There is a charm in the
very season of the year when this event occurred.   The variation of the Calendar never
disturbs its connection with the spring: and
the spring, whether in England or America,
is always beautiful, always full of hope.   The
whole scene of the Ascension is rich in encouragement.   This was evidently felt by the
Apostles, though we are surprised that it could
be so.   It is part of that *cheerfulness* of the
Acts of the Apostles, which we noted in the
last lecture as characteristic of this book.   We
trace this feature in it from the very first.
Though bereaved as no men ever were bereaved before (for they had lost from earthly
sight such a friend as no men had ever lost
before) the Apostles returned " with great
joy."   Such a state of feeling, the existence

of which we perceive on combining together what St Luke says at the end of his "former treatise" and the beginning of the second, quite startles us as we pass over the transition-line from the Gospel history: and this contrast of feeling is one of the points of connection on which we ought to dwell for contrast is a true connection, if by previous statements we have been led to look for it.

All this gives forth a very special claim for the observance of Ascension Day: and the claim comes upon us with additional force, if we view the Ascension as a binding together of the Gospels and the Acts, as a testimony to the coherence of Scripture. I know not how the day is observed in this country. In England we have larger congregations on this day than we used to have; there is a deeper feeling on the subject through the land; in our Cathedrals we have more music appropriate to the Festival; the conviction is stronger that the compilers of our Prayer Book showed a true instinct in appointing special portions of the service to mark the day when

our Lord "in the sight of all the Apostles as-
cended up into heaven to prepare a place for
us, that where He is, thither we might also
ascend, and reign with Him in glory." We all
know the value of embodying a principle in an
institution. Your Thanksgiving Day is a great
institution, as I had an opportunity of observing, when I was in America before This is
one of the Thanksgiving Days of the Catholic
Church; and its careful observance is a perpetual assertion of a cardinal truth, while it
impresses us with a deeper consciousness of
the evidential value of the Acts of the Apostles

From the Ascension of Christ let us now
look back in thought to *the Resurrection of
Christ*. In another way this great fact is a
strong link (in a very true sense it may be
said to be the strongest link) between the
Gospels and the Acts. The Ascension is sub-
ordinate to the Resurrection. The Ascension,
in fact, may very correctly be viewed as the
culminating point of the Resurrection — as
merely an essential part of it, however truly

it has a distinctive character of its own,
worthy of separate commemoration In the
very nature of the case the Resurrection must
be *consummate* in its importance. Think of
what it is that one should rise from the dead.
Even now, with the light of Christianity round
us, and the faith of all the past Christian ages
resting upon us, we find a difficulty in be-
lieving it. What a feeling of wonder and per-
plexity there was in the minds of the disciples,
in regard to this subject, during the Gospel
time! What confidence there is in the same
minds here! But a true connection between
two consecutive parts of the Bible resides in
this change What was said above of *contrast*
in regard to the Ascension is still more true
and forcible here in regard to the Resurrection.
A conviction of the truth of the Resurrection
sends a thrill through the whole Book of the
Acts, and gives to it life and expression and
power. Can any thing be more incredible than
that a mere delusion, a mere sentimental hys-
teria, should have communicated such nerve
to the book, such meaning to all its chapters,

such vigor to its words, such strong consistency to the Acts it records? The very form,
the very substance of the book is a testimony
to the fact of the Resurrection: and surely we
may argue conversely, that, if we believe this
fact, our faith rightly diffuses a feeling of radi-
ant confidence over the whole of the book.

To make this instinctive impression more
definite, and to give a reason for it, let us
look at some of the facts of the case I take
eight instances, four relating to the work of
Peter, four relating to that of Paul They
are drawn from the midst of occasions and
scenes extremely different from one another:
yet they are all harmonious in the unity of
the great truth I am noting I will name them
in chronological order, adding such reflections
as they naturally suggest.

Hear how on the day of Pentecost St. Peter
speaks of the Resurrection! He has been
quoting one of the Psalms of David. "Thou
wilt not leave my soul in hell, neither wilt
thou suffer thine Holy One to see corruption."
This, says Peter before all the people, can

not refer to David   That prophet's tomb was
near them, perhaps in their very sight, as
Peter preached.   "This the prophet spoke,"
said Peter, "of the resurrection of Christ, that
His soul was not left in hell, neither *His* flesh
did see corruption: this Jesus hath God raised
up, whereof we all are witnesses" What I
mark here is St Peter's confident and complete
theological teaching on the subject.   Once he
had been full of all sorts of doubts and diffi-
culties in reference to this question, and even
he had been guilty of disrespectful expostulation with his Lord, when He predicted His
dying and rising again   Now the whole theological range of the subject seemed present
to his mind and to be held with the firm
grasp of unhesitating conviction.   He had
often heard his Master quote the Old Testament   Now he does the same.   This is a
topic on which it is well worth while to
pause very carefully.   Is it not evident that
the promise has been fulfilled—that the Holy
Spirit has "taken of the things of Christ and
shown them unto him"—that "all things have

been brought to his remembrance, whatever Christ had spoken to him"?

Now turn to another occasion, which speedily followed. Peter and John have been together in the Temple; and there, at the public gate, in the name of Christ, have healed a man who was lame from his birth. This appearance of these two disciples side by side, here and afterwards on the mission to Samaria, is itself an expression of the harmony of the Acts with the Epistles To-gether they had been in the first interview with Jesus near the Jordan. Together they had been with Him among the nets on the Sea of Tiberias. Probably they were companions when the disciples were sent forth two and two. Certainly they were selected as companions, when preparation was to be made for the Passover. Certainly they were together immediately after the Resurrection and again at the solemn moment of the pastoral commission Their friendship is a most touching part of the Gospel history; and we are struck by the naturalness, so to speak, of

their appearing here together at the opening
of the apostolic history. The point before us
is their assertion regarding the Resurrection,
to which certainly they were able to bear
special testimony. "Ye denied the Holy One
and the Just, and desired a murderer to be
granted unto you; and killed the Prince of life,
whom God hath raised from the dead; whereof we are witnesses" These were their words
in Solomon's Porch How different had the
conduct of these two disciples been, soon
after the time when the last mention of Solomon's Porch occurred ! How full of fear were
they then ! How unflinching in courage are
they now ! And as we pursue the narrative,
we find that the Sadducees, "vexed that these
men were teaching the people and preaching
through Jesus the resurrection from the dead,"
brought them before the authorities; and still
the same confident language is used: "Be it
known unto you, that by the name of Jesus
Christ of Nazareth, whom ye crucified, whom
God raised from the dead, even by Him doth
this man stand before you whole," and it is

added, with great emphasis, that "they *marked the boldness* of Peter and John" We remember how it had been with these two Apostles, a short time before, in connection with the suffering, the death, and resurrection of Christ. Both had slept in the Garden of the Agony: both had forsaken the Lord in fear, and Peter had done worse: both, when the news came of the open tomb, had been filled with fear and doubt. Now the change is marvellous. Their fearless confidence is so great that nothing could surpass it; and Peter, in witnessing of the Resurrection, as truly proves by his new courage the power of the Holy Ghost, as he had proved it by his theological teaching on this great subject.

Before long a fresh series of incidents succeed, but still with the same witnessing to the truth of the Resurrection of Christ Many miracles were wrought by the Apostles, so as to produce a solemn and reverential awe among those who beheld them, Peter being named as the central figure in these scenes. Again the Sadducees are filled with "indig-

nation", and the Apostles are put in prison.
They are miraculously delivered and return to
their office of public teaching   When brought
before the Council, we read that Peter and
the other Apostles "answered and said We
ought to obey God rather than man. the God
of our fathers raised up Jesus, whom ye slew
and hanged on a tree. Him hath God raised
with His right hand to be a Prince and a Saviour . . . and we are witnesses of these
things " The thoughts which this scene brings
into the mind are somewhat different from the
thoughts suggested by the preceding   Then
we saw St Peter in companionship with his
early friend St John· the biographies of the
two men are blended together, as we have
seen them blended on earlier occasions; and
Peter appears, with his friend, as the great example of courage.   Now we see Peter with the
general group of the Apostles, their spokes-
man, their representative, witnessing, in their
name as well as his own, to the Resurrection
of Christ.   This truth is to be the doctrine,
the living power, the assuring comfort, of the

Universal Church. This testimony is the assertion of the great Catholic truth, which we proclaim in such glorious words at the close of the Nicene Creed: "I *look for* the resurrection of the dead, and the life of the world to come"

The last instance selected from the testimony of Peter concerning the Resurrection deserves peculiar attention. They are the words addressed to Cornelius " Him God raised from the dead and showed Him openly—not to all the people, but to witnesses chosen before of God—even to us," he adds, "who did eat and drink with Him after He rose from the dead." I can imagine a question arising in thoughtful minds, when we read here that Jesus Christ, after His Resurrection, was not shown openly to all the people, but only to select witnesses. Is not this somewhat strange? it might be asked. Is not the evidence of the Resurrection in this way somewhat attenuated? Was not the effect of this great event upon the minds of the people made somewhat less than it might otherwise have been? I think

hat a little reflection will show that there is
error in these thoughts. The very fact that
no public recognition of the risen Saviour is
recorded, though at first it might seem to
detract from the evidence of His Resurrection, now really serves to enhance it· for it
shows how free the witnesses of this event
were from a disposition to make their case
stronger than it was in fact. And, after all,
the conviction of mankind in all ages, as to
this fact, must rest on the testimony of a
few at this particular time But chiefly I
think we should remember that this reserved
manifestation to a few chosen disciples, appointed to be His witnesses afterwards, was
more in keeping with the dignity and glory of
the risen Saviour, which would now have been
lowered and made common by that promiscu-
ous and unrestricted intercourse with men,
which was necessary to His previous ministry. One feeling which we ought to foster
with the utmost care, in the contemplation
of this great event, is the feeling of solemnity
and reverence, and this is promoted by the

manner in which the Lord manifested Himself
after the Resurrection to St. Peter and a chosen
few Provision has been made, not only for
our belief in the Resurrection, but for our think-
ing of it in the right manner: and this fact
has, to the Christian mind, a strong evidential
force.

The four instances of testimony to Christ's
Resurrection, selected from St. Paul's life, may
be more rapidly enumerated, and a rapid enumeration brings all the more distinctly to view
the extraordinary variety of scene and circumstance in the midst of which this unwavering
testimony is consistently traced.

First there is the witness in the synagogue
of Antioch in Pisidia, a country town in the
centre of Asia Minor. After a historical and
prophetical preamble, similar to that in St Stephen's speech (and we must remember that he
had heard that speech) the Resurrection of
Christ is the point to which St. Paul steadily
works onward. He quotes the same Psalm
which St Paul quoted at Pentecost This
too is a correspondence to be well marked.

He puts in sharp contrast before his hearers what man had done in regard to Christ, and what God had done. "When they had fulfilled all that was written of Him, they took Him down from the tree and laid Him in a sepulchre: but God raised Him from the dead the promise that was made unto the fathers, God hath fulfilled the same unto us their children, in that He hath raised up Jesus again" We should observe too how he says· "He was seen many days of them which came up with Him from Galilee to Jerusalem, who are His witnesses unto the people" This mention of Galilee is significant, as we shall see afterwards. He knits here his testimony with theirs: and in so doing (we may lawfully add) he knits together the Acts and the Epistles

The seventeenth chapter of this book contains two very marked and two very distinct examples of St. Paul's testimony to the Resurrection. At Thessalonica the occasion was perhaps not very different from that which has been noticed at Antioch in Pisidia. The

5

scene to which our attention is called is still
a synagogue. The place, however, and the
character of the population by which St Paul
is now surrounded, is very different. He has
now crossed from Asia into Europe: the great
council and the public meeting with St. Peter
have taken place; and he is now in a great em-
porium of commerce by the sea Still we observe that his testimony is unchanged and
unwavering. Still it is the Resurrection of
Christ which gives living power to his words,
bringing to conversion those who were afterwards addressed in the Epistles to the Thes-
salonians, and in the case of others resulting in
the persecution which urged the Apostle onward to Berea, and thence to Athens.

Turning now to this new scene we find ourselves entirely removed from the old doc-
trinal ground which was taken in addressing
the Jews. The Apostle's argument is now not
theological but philosophical. Still, however,
it is the Resurrection from the dead which "in
the market place" causes the commotion in
the minds of the Stoics and Epicureans. " He

seemeth to be a setter-forth of strange gods,
because he preached unto them Jesus and the
Resurrection " Still it is the same topic which
closes the great speech on Areopagus. "God
hath appointed a day in the which He will
judge the world in righteousness by that Man
whom He hath ordained, whereof He hath
given assurance unto all men, in that He hath
raised Him from the dead—and when they
heard of the Resurrection of the dead, some
mocked; and others said, We will hear thee
again of this matter."

The last selected occasion is that on which
Paul stood before Festus and Agrippa. It is
very startling to think of him as proclaiming
before the Roman Governor the Resurrection
of one whom Pilate, that officer's predecessor,
had crucified. Contrast does indeed here form
a vivid connection between the Gospels and
the Acts. Leaving on one side all that was
especially addressed to Agrippa regarding the
Resurrection, let us pass at once to the culminating point of the speech: " Having obtained
help of God I continue unto this day, wit-

nessing both to small and great, that Christ
should suffer and that He should be the
first that should rise from the dead" At
this point occurs the sudden incredulous interruption of Festus: "Paul, thou art beside thyself: much learning hath made thee
mad"—with the Apostle's famous reply· "I
am not mad, most noble Festus, but speak
forth the words of truth and soberness." The
Roman officer could not understand St Paul's
enthusiasm or his belief in the Resurrection.
What, however, is especially suggested to us
at this point is the combination of this en-
thusiastic belief with the utmost sobriety of
character. No one can study the records of
St Paul's life without observing his strong
good sense and his freedom from fanaticism.
That to such a man faith in Christ's Resurrection should have been the living power
which moved and directed his conduct is a
fact to arrest any thoughtful mind.

But, to return to the remark made above,
what a variety of incident is here ! what a succession of scenes and persons to stimulate our

thought! what an animated and diversified history! Yet how strong and fresh flows the stream of steady and uniform assertion of the Resurrection of Christ! And is it not quite evident that both Apostles attested what they personally knew to be true, one from what he had personally seen, the other from what eye-witnesses had told him? *The evidence is contemporary.* On the edge of this stream of testimony we find ourselves in all varieties of scenery: but the living stream that flows past is one

Some have laboriously brought together all the tendencies of thought, the accidental movements of opinion, the inevitable social changes, which before the close of the second century combined in forming Christianity and the Christian Church. There is no reason to deny these tendencies or the reality of these progressive changes. But add them all together: and they do not explain Christianity and the Church. The living power is wanting. As well might we explain physical life by enumerating and describing gelatine and fibrine, lime and oxygen, and the like   These ingredients are there, with the laws which operate on them and control them, but all together they do not make the living man   something is still wanting which baffles science.   So it is here with the criticism which leaves out the Resurrection. It can analyze the ingredients: but it cannot explain the life.   It seems to me, too, that this fresh early spirit of strong belief, which we have seen alike in St. Peter and St Paul, could not have been represented naturally by a late compiler or by an inventor   It would have been impossible either to have forged it or reproduced it.   The very *manner* in which the Resurrection was proclaimed joins together by an indissoluble bond the Acts and the Gospels.

As we have moved back already from the Ascension to the Resurrection, so let us now move back from the Resurrection to the earthly life, to *the works and words of Christ.*   For this purpose we may be content to fix our position in one single place.   We will take our stand upon the narrative of the Conversion of

Cornelius, and limit ourselves to that ground. Previously—in the last lecture—we took a survey of this ground in its tendency to establish the artless veracity of the Acts. Now I invite attention to it for a different reason I think I see in this section of the history three places of close organic connection between the Acts and the Gospel-events. They are all parts of the living experience of St Peter: which indeed is precisely what we should look for. We should perhaps hardly expect any evidence of this kind in connection with St. Paul. He had never lived with Christ But with Peter personal memories of the Lord must have been ever in his mind; and we are instinctively prepared for indications of them to appear. The order in which we consider these three indications is of little moment. I will take the earliest first, then the latest, then the intermediate one

Our Lord once spoke a parable to this effect: "Not that which entereth into a man, by his mouth, defileth him: but that which cometh from within, out of the heart, that

defileth the man." We know the meaning of
this parable, as regards the superstition of
mere outward things on the one hand, and
the terrible pollution of sin in the heart on
the other But the parable has a wide range
beyond the mere individual, and lays down
the broad universal basis upon which religious
communion in the Church of Christ is built.
In our general recollection of the parable there
is nothing to associate it specially with Peter,
or to suggest any intimate link here between
the Gospels and the Acts But on reading
carefully we soon see its personal connection
with this Apostle; and critical inquiry reveals
the link which in this place connects the
Gospels and the Acts.

Both St Matthew and St Mark tell us that
the disciples afterwards privately asked the
meaning of the parable But one of them in-
forms us of the place where this conversation
occurred; the other tells us who asked the
question that led to Christ's answer. St. Matthew says that it was " when He was entered
into the house from the people " that this pri-

vate conversation took place That was the
house of Simon and Andrew But St Mark
tells us (observe that it is St Mark) of something more definite and personal " Peter said
unto Him, Declare unto us this parable " Peter, as usual, is ready with his words, and while
honestly, doubtless, eager for instruction, is
impetuous and impatient We may thank him
for this 'eagerness and impetuosity, for it has
brought down to us from that conversation
at Capernaum the most solemn of all warnings,
that foul desires, which come from within, de-
file us morally and spiritually.

Here is the connection with St Peter. and
even this is a bond between the Acts and the
Gospels; for we have thus vividly before us the
personality of the man who was appointed to
secure the conversion of Cornelius. But exact
criticism reveals to us, in this conversation
at Capernaum, a distinct organic connection
with that great subsequent occurrence. For
according to the true reading of the manuscripts, what St. Mark adds at the close of this
Gospel story is as follows: "This He said—

this the Lord said—*cleansing all meats*—pro-
nouncing all meats pure " It was an anticipation—a strictly verbal anticipation—of what
was said at Joppa—" What the Lord *hath
cleansed*, that call not thou common." We
often blame the critics; but we have frequently
good reason to thank them. The fact of the
true reading may be stated very confidently.
And can we doubt that a remembrance of his
Lord's words came into St Peter's mind in connection with the case of Cornelius, if not with
the flash of a sudden conviction, yet with a
gradual and in the end irresistible persuasion,
during the vision at Joppa, or in conversation
at Cæsarea ? The Lord had spoken the words
in answer to a pointed question The question
too had been asked by himself It had been
asked too and answered in that house, which had
been familiar to him from early days, and which
must ever have seemed full of the presence
and instruction of Christ We should note,
too, that the identical Greek word for cleansing, or declaring pure, is employed in the
two cases. Finally we must observe that this

general remark concerning the Lord's meaning in the parable is found in St Mark, in
that Evangelist who was termed in the early
Church "the interpreter of Peter" In order
to establish quite confidently the reality of
this connection, we have only, it seems to
me, to take into account the ordinary laws and
operations and associations of human thought.
And yet the connection is delicate and subtle,
not likely to have come into existence in the
development of a vague late tradition; and
not likely to have been the invention of a
forger; for a forger thinks of that which is
palpable and obviously adapted to strike his
reader immediately.

I now turn to a second bond of connection
between this part of the Acts of the Apostles
and passages of the Gospel history   In one portion of the narrative of the Conversion of Cornelius St Peter distinctly says that he went
through a conscious reminiscence   When the
crisis came, when the Holy Ghost fell upon
those who were assembled in the house of
Cornelius, "then," says Peter to the Apostles

and Elders, before whom he is defending himself, " *then remembered I* the word of the Lord,
how He said, John indeed baptized with water:
but ye shall be baptized with the Holy Ghost "
I referred in my last lecture to this artless
statement of a conscious reminiscence as an
indication of natural truthfulness in the history
of the Acts   Now I refer to it for a different
reason, for the purpose of calling attention to
the fact that we here have a specimen of
natural *organic* connection, so to speak, between the Acts and the Gospels. It is true
indeed that the words most nearly resembling
those which St Peter says that he remembered
on this occasion, are found in the first chapter
of the Acts themselves   But other words,
nearly identical, were spoken by our Lord on
other occasions.   One part of His training was
clearly to connect in the minds of the disciples
the remembrance of John the Baptist and the
expectation of Pentecost   Thus we are at this
point, so to speak, on a line of communication
which runs through more parts than one of the
Gospels and more parts than one of the Acts.

But I am especially laying stress here on the value of this personal reminiscence, as establishing a link of biographical connection between these two parts of the New Testament. There is something wonderfully vivid in Peter's account of his recollection We call to mind indeed what St Paul said at Miletus of "remembering the word of the Lord Jesus, how He said, It is more blessed to give than to receive" But there is a difference in the tone and feeling of the two occurrences; and I think it is easy to see in the one case and not in the other the direct action of personal memory St. Paul quotes what had been related to him St Peter gives the words which his own ears had heard. The Apostles too, who were listening to him, had heard the same words spoken. The argument must thus have been of the weightiest kind; and it had an immediate effect. How far this kind of reference to the past is likely to have been introduced into a document not authentic, I must ask thoughtful men to judge. To my mind what we read here has

an air of thorough reality and naturalness, so
that I see before me here a rivet, so to speak,
strong and unmovable between the Gospels
and the Acts

In this instance St John the Baptist is
named. So it is in the third instance, to
which I now turn   I shall have occasion to
revert to the Baptist again, before the conclusion of this lecture   Let me ask attention
to the words which Peter is recorded to have
addressed to Cornelius " That word ye know,
that went through all Judea, beginning from
Galilee, after the baptism which John preached,
Jesus of Nazareth, how God anointed Him
with the Holy Ghost and with power, who
went about doing good. . . . and we are witnesses of those things " "*Who went about doing
good*" There is extraordinary beauty in this
phrase; and note that it is Peter who uses it—
Peter, who had been with Jesus from the first
Peter, who saw all those Galilean miracles   I
do not think that St Paul would have said precisely this. We should hardly expect it from
him, for he had not lived day by day in perso-

nal intercourse with Christ. Just so I do not think St. Paul would have written what we find in St Peter's first epistle: "Whom not having seen ye love" Peter had seen and had heard, while in both cases he is addressing those who had not seen and heard In each case the language is perfectly true to nature. In each case our confidence grows as we read and study. In each case Palestine is the truthful background of what is immediately before us. In the instance under our particular consideration here, there is both the charm of surprise, and the suggestion of most solemn thought We perceive how Capernaum connects itself by a Divine prearrangement with Cæsarea

I believe we might follow the same method of inquiry further and find other examples of visible association with the Gospel-time, even if we were to limit ourselves to the occurrences connected with Cornelius. Does it not naturally strike us that in what was said and done in reference to the centurion at Capernaum there was an anticipation of certain things that regard the centurion at Cæsarea, and a latent

instruction likely to revive in St Peter's mind ?
Prejudices are not easily loosened, but they
may be loosened gradually and imperceptibly,
and preparation may be made long beforehand
for a change of mind and conduct very decided,
when it comes   It is difficult to believe that
St. Peter can have been brought to his conclusion at Cæsarea without calling to mind
the centurion whose servant was healed at Capernaum.   The admirable character of the two
men must have produced similar impressions
upon his mind.   The testimony, too, of the
Jews was remarkably similar in the two cases
In the former instance they besought the Lord
earnestly that He would grant the centurion's
request, "saying that he was worthy for whom
He should do this, for he loveth our nation,
and hath built us a synagogue"   In the latter
instance the messengers who came from Cæsarea to Joppa bear testimony to Peter that
Cornelius is "a just man, and one that fear-
eth God, and of a good report among all the
nation of the Jews"   Nothing could be more
likely to prepare Peter for the work which he

was destined to do afterwards at Cæsarea than the occurrence which took place at Capernaum He had heard his Lord say of a heathen soldier that " He had not found so great faith, no, not in Israel, and that many should come from the East and West, and sit down with Abraham and Isaac and Jacob, in the kingdom of God " And now the Lord had taught him, through the operation of the Holy Spirit and through providential guiding, what these words meant for the whole world; choosing him as the instrument for beginning the great change in the history of mankind.

But I pass now to another of those interconnections between the Gospels and the Acts of the Apostles, which are not very obtrusive at first sight, but which, when observed, have an argumentative value in such an inquiry as the present. I find this in *the frequent mention of Galilee* in the earlier part of the Acts of the Apostles, and in *the manner* of its mention Even St Paul names Galilee when addressing the Jews in the synagogue at Antioch in Pisidia; and this, I think, is worthy of ob-

6

servation. "God raised Him from the dead; and He was seen many days of them which came up with Him *from Galilee* to Jerusalem; who are His witnesses unto the people." There is an echo of the Gospel-time in this mention of Galilee: and occurring, as it does, in a speech by St Paul in Asia Minor, it is, as I have said, worthy of observation. Probably up to this time he had had very little to do with Galilee Afterwards, indeed, he was in its close neighborhood, when he spent two years at Cæsarea, and then it is quite possible that he cooperated with Luke in gathering together notices of Gospel incidents connected with Galilee; but that part of this Apostle's life was not yet come. Thus this local framing of his Gospel instruction is remarkable; and I think we do not transgress the bounds of reasonable speculation, if we fancy that we see here a result of that early fortnight, spent in close communion by St Paul and St. Peter together, of which I have spoken above. Certainly they conversed of the Resurrection Certainly they conversed of Galilee

With St. Peter himself the reminiscence of Galilee was the most intimate kind that is possible   The local influences that surrounded him from the first, the character that originally belonged to him, were Galilean   His early training too, under Christ, was in Galilee   There he had learned to know and love his Master.   There he had listened to His discourses   There he had been a witness of His miracles   Part of his Master's reproach too, which it was his glory to bear, was connected with this despised region.   If the proud question was asked: "Doth Christ come out of Galilee ? ' it was natural that the disciple should be asked· "Art thou also of Galilee ?"   This being so, it is interesting and important to observe how the remembrance of Galilee colors both the later associations of Peter with Christ in the Gospel-time, and also the earlier parts of the Apostolic history —for consistency between these two consecutive parts of the New Testament is confirmed by the continuous and natural use of a geographical term   This mark is indelibly fixed

on the sad story of the denial· "Thou art a
Galilean· thy speech betrayeth thee" The
same allusion is mingled with the joy of the
Resurrection "Tell His disciples and Peter,
that He goeth before you into Galilee." The
renewed lesson drawn from the fisherman's
craft, the command to feed the sheep and
lambs of Christ, were given in Galilee And
turning now to the Acts of the Apostles, we
find Galilee made conspicuous at three very
marked moments of St Peter's life; and, we
may add, made naturally conspicuous, without any suspicion of ingenious design On
Mount Olivet when the disciples are gazing
upward, the words of the angel are, "Ye
men of Galilee, why stand ye gazing up into
heaven!" How these words seem to connect together this great consummation with
the early days of Bethsaida and Cana! At
the outpouring of the Holy Ghost, the ex-
clamation was, "Are not all these which
speak Galileans?" And now again, at the
other great critical moment of Peter's mission
to the world, he sets the Gospel before Cor-

nelius as "the word which was published throughout all Judea, and *began from Galilee*" It seems to us that it was hardly needful to have named Galilee on this occasion; but the old days came back upon Peter's memory as he spoke, and he could not omit the allusion, when speaking of Him "who went about doing good" At the second Pentecost, as at the first, the speaker who stands before us is still "the pilot of the Galilean lake." We must not exaggerate the importance of a consistency of this kind Its argumentative value consists partly in the fact that it is very natural, and partly in its power of easy combination with other evidences of the same kind. This remark too may be permitted, that in the Apocryphal Acts there is apt to be a hierarchical complexion, corresponding with the late date at which they were composed, whereas we have here blowing over us the fresh healthy air of the early companionship with Jesus.

Another very important subject in the interlacing, so to speak, of the Acts with the Epistles, is the occurrence of *the mention of*

John the Baptist   If the name of that Great
Forerunner of Christ had not occurred at all
in the Book of the Acts, such a circumstance
might have been suspicious. And yet now
that these preparatory days are over, and the
Gospel is entering upon its mature mission,
a too prominent mention of the Baptist might
in another way have excited suspicion   In
this matter again we must take into account
the words both of St Peter and of St. Paul.
The grand shadow of the Baptist is thrown
over the whole range of·the Acts of the Apostles   As to the mention of the Great Forerunner in connection with St Paul's life and
work, two circumstances are worthy of remark, because they are perfectly natural   It
was probable, from the character and noto-
riety of John's preaching, that traces of his
discipleship would be found in distant places,
affected partly by the return of pilgrims who
had heard him in Palestine, partly by the diffusion of his influence through intermediate
channels   And this we do find, and in places
very likely for such discipleship to be promi-

nent, namely in Alexandria and Ephesus We
remember how Apollos, who came from the
former place, "knew only the baptism of
John," and how, when more fully instructed
by St. Paul's friends, Aquila and Priscilla, he
passed on to Corinth, to exercise a most useful
ministry there We remember too how Paul
himself soon afterwards encountered at Ephesus "certain disciples," as they are termed,
who "knew only John's baptism" All this
is perfectly natural; and just so far it tends to
bind together the Acts and the Gospels, that
we find in the Gospels the explanation of
what we read here in the Acts The other
point of interest is this, that when St Paul,
names this subject, he employs his own characteristic style He is well acquainted with
the Mission of John the Baptist, he knows the
Gospel in its prelude, and of this prelude he
apprehends the full importance The Baptist's Mission is part of his teaching, when
he speaks to unconverted Jews We should
hardly expect this topic to.appear in his Epistles written to organized Christian Churches

But in the synagogue at Antioch in Pisidia
he opens the Gospel-message thus. "God according to His promise hath raised unto Israel
a Saviour, Jesus, whom John had preached
before his coming the baptism of repentance
to all the people of Israel." But, as I have
said, St Paul uses here his characteristic style.
"As John fulfilled his course, he said, whom
think ye that I am? I am not He. But be-
hold there cometh One after me, whose shoes
of His feet I am not worthy to loose" *"As
John fulfilled his course"* It is a metaphor
from the footrace in the Greek games. This is
his way of expressing energy, directness and
perseverance. It is just the language which
he uses of himself, both elsewhere in the Acts
and in the Epistles. "I count not my life
dear unto myself, that I might *finish my course*
with joy"; and again—"*I have finished my
course:* I have kept the faith" It is most interesting thus to see blended together the
lively imagery of the Greek games and the
very words uttered in the wilderness and by
the banks of the Jordan—to see the Great

Forerunner and the Apostle of the Gentiles, as it were, side by side   .

In Peter's reference to John the Baptist the interest is of a different kind. In this case there is the freshness of a personal recollection. " *Then remembered I* the word of the Lord, how He said, John indeed baptized with water: but ye shall be baptized with the Holy Ghost " He describes his own state of mind. Paul could not have said this. He had not heard what Christ the Lord said of John: and at Antioch in Pisidia he was addressing those who had not directly heard, though the fame of John the Baptist had reached them. Just so there is the life of a personal recollection in the words used to Cornelius: " That word ye know, which was published throughout all Judea, and began from Galilee, *after the baptism which John preached.*" I have already remarked on this sentence as regards the mention of Galilee. Now let us observe it as regards the mention of John the Baptist. If not literally a disciple of the Baptist, it was within the range

of the Baptist's influence, and apparently in
his actual presence, that Peter had his first
interview with Christ and received his new
name.   Nor are these the only instances, in
the Acts of the Apostles, where we find Peter
making allusion to those early days, to which
his later days were bound by gradually grow-
ing and expanding experience   He says at
the very outset, when a successor to Judas is
to be chosen   "Of these men that have com-
panied with us all the time that the Lord
Jesus went in and out among us, *beginning
from the baptism of John*, unto that same
day that He was taken up from us, must one
be ordained to be a witness with us of the
resurrection "

The retrospect of the Gospel-time, which,
standing on the ground of the Acts of the
Apostles, we have thus taken, from the Ascension of Christ to the mission of John the Baptist, suggests a thought that should be very
present to our minds, when we are considering the relation of these two portions of
our early sacred history.   The Gospel-time

was a period of training for the Apostles. This fact gives to us a principle of continuity of which we ought never to lose sight. With this fact fresh in our memories we trace connection in various instances where otherwise it would not be perceived. It is one thing to read the Gospels, as of course we do read them, for perpetual and direct instruction; quite another thing to see in the words and incidents recorded there a schooling of the Apostles for that future work, select specimens of which are given in the Book of Acts. The links which we trace by this method may, in some cases, be minute, but perhaps they are all the more valuable on that very account. They may not be clear to the eye at first sight, but this really enhances their testimony if only they are distinctly visible when they are discovered.

And we observe that, on this view of the matter, *Peter* is the personal link which chiefly binds together the early part of the Acts of the Apostles with the Evangelic history. This must, in the nature of the case, be so Peter

is in the Evangelic record the most conspicuous person among the disciples of Christ.
Whatever training the other Apostles received
was concentrated, as it were, in him. And on
the other side, Peter is the conspicuous figure
on the canvas on all the early part of the Acts
of the Apostles The primitive formation of
the Church, so far as it is recorded, is personi-
fied, as it were, in him Hence in travelling
along the line of his personal biography we
pass easily from the one ground to the other.
Does not the devout mind feel instinctively
that we have here the proofs both of a natural
truthfulness and of a divine prearrangement?

In this way we are led to do more justice
to St Peter than has always been accorded
to him. In modern times, as it seems to me,
the claims of this great Apostle on our theological and literary work have been in some
degree overlooked. There was indeed a period, when, for long ages, Peter was placed
upon a solitary pinnacle which he was never
intended to occupy During the last half century, throughout the Reformed parts of Chris-

tendom, there have been profuse illustrations of the life and character and work of St Paul. Meanwhile the life and character and work of St Peter have been somewhat in the shade. The time seems now to be come for some compensation for this comparative neglect, some correcting of this anomaly The true relative position of Peter and Paul is side by side; and in no way do we become more conscious of this than when we remember that these two inspired men are respectively the links between the Acts of the Apostles with the Gospels on the one side and with the Epistles on the other.

This leads to a concluding remark. I have said that the true relation of Peter and Paul is side by side. In this book we see them placed thus together. One great feature of the Book of the Acts is that it is the meeting ground of these two Apostles I spoke in my last lecture of the view held by some that there was not only a long-continued antagonism in the Church between the School of St Peter and the School of St. Paul, but a sharp antagonism between these two Apostles themselves, and that this book was put together at a comparatively late period with a partisan purpose and to indicate a supposed reconciliation   The theory takes different forms; or rather there are more theories than one, some being contradictions of the rest   And it seems to me that it would be very easy to construct diverse theories of this kind and to put explanations on various parts of this book accordingly   The simplest explanation, however, is the best   The old true representation of this subject will live and edify the world, when a great variety of new speculations have had their day.   The result of these speculations, and of their conflict with one another, will be to make men realize more and more the inspired unity of St. Peter and St. Paul.   Whatever antagonism there may have been among those who used their names, *it never had their sanction.* They meet in this book, not, like Laban and Jacob, for a great separation, but for perpetual and sacred union   At the Apostolic Council, which may be termed the central place in this book, we see them hand in hand. They are one in faith, one in love, one in mutual confidence, one in the proclamation of great principles The Acts of the Apostles assert the same unanimity, as that which we find asserted in the Epistles. "Whether it were I or they, so we preached and so ye believed."

LECTURE III.

THE BOOK OF THE ACTS IN CONNECTION WITH THE APOSTOLIC EPISTLES

LECTURE III.

THE BOOK OF THE ACTS IN CONNECTION WITH THE APOSTOLIC EPISTLES

WHEN it had been decided that I was to deliver these lectures, and I began to revolve their substance and arrangement in my mind, the thought of my early boyhood came vividly over me. I recalled that western part of Yorkshire, with its green open pastures, its gray limestone cliffs, its trout streams and hazel woods, where I used then to live. And with this memory fresh and active, it seemed to me the strangest thing in the world that I should be preparing to lecture here, on the opposite side of the Atlantic. Fifty years ago, when even railroads were hardly known, the separation caused by the Ocean had a reality, especially to rural people, which now has almost ceased to be appreciable.

Why do I make this personal allusion? Not, I hope, from a feeling of personal importance, as regards myself, but for a good and sufficient reason. That village in Craven, the western district of Yorkshire, was the native place of Paley. Over those green pastures he used to wander Up those limestone cliffs he used to climb Those •hazel woods and trout streams were as familiar to him, when he was a boy, as to me when I was a boy. His father in extreme old age was my father's schoolmaster I was brought up, when a child, in the midst of anecdotes of Paley and his family It is not then unnatural that I should take a peculiar interest in his works

Of the three great works of Paley, the " Moral Philosophy," the " Evidences of Christianity," and the " Horæ Paulinæ," the last mentioned is by far the most original and the most permanently valuable : and it has a special value even on this account, that it is eminently characteristic of the man. Never

did an author more truly reproduce himself
than Paley in this book He was singularly
fond of circumstantial evidence. When he was
a young man, it was his delight to spend much
time in law courts, listening to the cross-examination of witnesses; and the method of
this book might correctly be termed a cross-
examination of St Luke and St Paul

But again this method of obtaining evidence
never loses its value, whatever changes may
take place in human opinion or human science Other kinds of argument in defence of
Christianity are forced to modify and adapt
themselves, as the human world advances.
But this method, in the nature of the case,
can never be obsolete Again some parts of
the argument in the "Horæ Paulinæ" may be
overstated, some may be erroneous But this
does not affect the rest In certain modes of
argumentation, if one part is unsound, all the
remainder falls with it Not so in this case.
There may be mistakes, here and there, in
specimens brought forward as "undesigned coincidences" But if they fall prostrate, the rest

stand upright   Moreover the example set by
Paley in this work can be imitated, as it has
been imitated, by others   It is surprising how
the Bible yields new results, if this mode of
inquiry is applied to its sacred pages.

Now it is to be observed that the *method*
of the "Horæ Paulinæ," the search for "undesigned coincidences,"—*i. e* , coincidences that
tend to prove the consistency of two things
which we are comparing, because they are
true coincidences, while yet they have not
been introduced by design,—this method is
often applicable to the comparison of *different
parts of the same document*, as well as the comparison of documents of different kinds   Paley's great task is to compare the Epistles of
St Paul with the Acts of the Apostles, so as
to bring to view points of agreement, in which
there is no suspicion of design, and thus to establish the independence, the authenticity, and
the honesty of the letters on the one hand,
and of the history on the other.   But the same
method might be applied to different parts of
the same letter.   In this way, especially if

the notices of person and place and circumstances are abundant enough to give good opportunity, forgery can often be detected. Paley himself deals in this manner with the Epistle to the Philippians, as regards the notice of Epaphroditus. How far he is quite successful in this particular instance is a question which we need not raise I am only illustrating a mode of procedure

This method is similarly applicable to various parts of the Acts of the Apostles, taken as one document by itself, and especially to two parts. The earlier of these was dealt with in my first lecture. There are two accounts of the Conversion of Cornelius; and I endeavored to show that in this case we have by no means to do with mere repetition, but that a minute comparison made with careful reference to the circumstances under which the two accounts are given, brings to view latent coincidences, which have escaped the notice of commentators. Peter tells his story under apologetic conditions· and the variations which we find in his story, while strictly in harmony with the other account, are just such as might be expected to occur under the circumstances of the case, while yet they show no trace of ingenious design This tends to give confidence in that part of the Acts of the Apostles But there is another part of the book, to which the same method is still more applicable There are three accounts of St Paul's Conversion, one given directly by St Luke in the ninth chapter, the others by St. Paul himself, as related in the twenty-second and twenty-sixth chapters, under apologetic conditions, but conditions extremely different from one another. Here then, in this threefold comparison, we have excellent opportunities for detecting forgery, if forgery exists, or for dispersing the mists of legend, if these accounts are legendary On the other hand, if we find variations in St Paul's mode of telling his story which involve no inconsistency with one another, or with St Luke's account, while yet they correspond with the character of the man and the circumstances in which he is placed, and while, at the same time there is clearly no contrivance in these differences and resemblances, then we acquire great confidence in the veracity of the book which is before us   Let us give a short time to this analysis, before we proceed to the remarks which arise on a general comparison of the Acts with the Epistles

The first apologetic statement by St Paul is before an angry mob in the Temple Court at Jerusalem, the second before Festus the Governor and Herod Agrippa II   In each case he is obliged to be polemical and yet persuasive   In each case he has to speak, under difficult circumstances, to hearers who are not very willing to be convinced   He himself terms these addresses "defences"   Hence we might expect that on these occasions certain things would be omitted, which, though important in the direct narrative, had at these times no apologetic value, and, on the other hand, that certain things would be added likely to be specially persuasive to the audiences respectively addressed. And this we find to be the case   Thus it was very impor-

tant, on both occasions, for St Paul to point
out the emphatic nature of *the miracle*.   Hence
he says that the light which appeared to him
was "a great light". he says that it was
"about noon"—"at mid-day"—and that it
exceeded the brightness even of the sun at
that time   Thus to the fact that the Apostle
was speaking apologetically on these occasions we are indebted for some information on
the subject, which otherwise we should not
possess   The omissions too in the accounts
given by St Paul are equally observable   It
has been correctly remarked that St Luke,
as is natural to a physician, observes symp-
toms, as for instance in the narrative of the
healing of the lame man at the Temple gate,
and the coming of blindness on Elymas at
Paphos   So, in his history of St Paul's Conversion, he mentions "the falling, as it were,
of scales" from the Apostle's eyes   But it
would have been beside the mark for St Paul
to have referred to this in either speech   Nor
would it have been to his purpose to have introduced the exact topographical details con-

nected with his conversion,—"the house of Judas" and the "Straight Street,"—or to have mentioned the fact that he spent "three days" without food, the naming of which things is quite natural to the direct historian. It will be seen at once, I believe, that we are here on a line of thought, which supplies a very decisive test as to the reality and truthfulness of what we read in the Acts of the Apostles concerning St Paul's Conversion

Let us now compare the defences with one another. Of course they have the apologetic character in common. and this we have considered   But, as I have said, they were spoken under circumstances extremely different. If they were true to the circumstances under which they are alleged to have been uttered, and true likewise to the character of the speaker as a man of good judgment and fine tact, they must exhibit corresponding variations   Speaking to the angry Jewish mob in the Temple Court, it was essential that St. Paul should be conciliatory, by presenting his subject as much as possible on the *Jewish*

side, and keeping back as long as possible
that mention of the Gentiles which was peculiarly offensive to them   This he does with
remarkable skill.   He has only a few moments
at his disposal, while he keeps the mob at
bay   But he employs these moments well.
He speaks in Hebrew: he uses the most
acceptable introduction, naming his hearers
"brethren and fathers".   he tells them that
he was nurtured in that selfsame Sacred City,
Jerusalem, where he is speaking. he tells them
that he was educated by that famous and
honored teacher, Gamaliel.   Were it not for
this speech, we should not have known that
St Paul was "brought up" in youth "at the
feet of Gamaliel."   He terms the law in which
he had been brought up "the law of the
fathers."   When he says that he was formerly
zealous in this cause, he adds "as ye all are
this day."   He says not simply, as St Luke
does, that he asked for letters to Damascus,
but that he obtained them, and that too (here
adding to St Luke) "from the whole body of
the elders," some of whom were probably

present at the moment When he speaks of
the persecuting Jews at Damascus, he calls
them "brethren"; and of Ananias he does
not say that he is a Christian brother or a
Christian disciple, but that he is "a man
pious according to the Jewish law": and he
adds, just as the messengers to Peter made a
similar addition regarding Cornelius, that "he
had a good report of all that dwelt there"
The coming of Ananias, and his standing
over him, and his own looking up into the
face of the visitor, should be noted as specimens of the vivid language of one who is
telling his own story Under this head of
vivid reminiscence may be classed too the
instinctive naming of *Damascus* four times in
the speech. The words in which Ananias is
quoted as saying "The God of our fathers
hath chosen thee" is, once more, an indication of the conciliatory skill with which the
Apostle speaks, as is his withholding the express mention of the Gentiles, when Ananias
says, "Thou shalt be His witness *unto all men*"
But especially we must mark the introducing

of his vision in the Temple, of which, but for this speech, we should have known nothing. In that very same sacred place where he was now standing, God had spoken to him and given him his commission to "the Gentiles" At that detested word the uproar began again, and they would hear him no longer But he had gained his point. He had told the story of his conversion to those who were most unwilling to listen Our part, as critics, in the scrutiny of this speech, is to observe how all the omissions, the additions, the variations of emphasis, on comparison with the direct narrative, fit the occasion, and also harmonize with what we know from other sources of St. Paul's versatility, tact, and presence of mind.

If next we turn to the speech before Festus and Agrippa, we find the story of his conversion told with what might be termed a strong *Gentile* coloring, and this was in harmony with the occasion and quite according to the tone and habit of St Paul's mind and character. Here he speaks under less constraint and with no fear of a violent interruption. Hence he

can take a wider scope and can dwell more
largely upon doctrine, and this he does ad-
mirably   A creed or a catechism might be
constructed from this speech at Cæsarea   He
has the religious interests of Festus, too, to
consider; and it is his duty so to speak as to
persuade him, if possible, as well as Agrippa
He appeals strongly to personal conscience
It is his best policy to take distinctively Christian ground   He says at the outset that
"*Jews*" are his accusers, and he adds, in a
later part of the speech, "for which hope's
sake I am accused by *Jews*." He speaks of
them as hostile to him, not as friends   He
places them, as it were, outside of the position on which he himself stands.   On the other
hand, he does identify himself with the Christians at Damascus, calling them "saints":
and he says that he endeavored to force them
"to blaspheme" No such language would
have been possible before the Jewish mob, or
at least, if he had used it, the interruption and
uproar would have been hastened.   The omissions too which we observe, on comparing

this speech with the other, are very significant, and thoroughly in accord with the contrast of the two occasions At Cæsarea he does not mention Ananias at all, on whom he had laid so much stress at Jerusalem—nor does he say any thing of his own vision in the Temple The authority of an obscure Jew of Damascus could have had no weight with Agrippa, and the mention of a vision might have provoked the ridicule of Festus Throughout we observe that the mission to the Gentiles is made conspicuous And to close this imperfect comparison of the two speeches by noticing one particular, which at first sight is very trivial, but which really contains a great deal of evidential force, he says here that the voice on the Damascus road spoke to him "in the Hebrew tongue" He did not state this while addressing the mob in the Temple Court, and for two reasons this difference is entirely natural He was then speaking in Hebrew: he is now speaking in Greek.

Now this dissection, if I may use such a term, of these parts of the Acts of the Apos-

tles, reveals the lineaments of an internal
structure, which are not apparent on the surface   It is like the dissection of a leaf, which
outwardly may seem very smooth and uniform,
but which within has vegetable fibre and
tissue, delicate but systematic, and giving
beauty and coherency to the whole   This
kind of evidence, too, if it can be sustained in
fact, is, I imagine, peculiarly strong. This I
infer from the determined way in which it
is neglected, or only very slightly noticed,
by those who have theories to construct regarding the origin and texture of the Acts of
the Apostles.   By developing out of our own
thoughts a bold general theory of the intention of this book, and by leaving out of view
the minute evidence of the facts of the case,
we might make any thing of the book   I will
give an illustration of what I mean.   One
writer (I am sorry to add that he is an English writer), assuming that the intention of
the author of the Acts is to establish for St.
Paul an honorable parallelism with the older
apostles, says this . " The personal appear-

8

ance of Christ to the older apostles being a
prominent feature," to balance this "the story
of the Conversion of St Paul is related three
times" Now what is the best mode of deal-
ing with a criticism of this kind? I imagine
that no plan is better than to show, by careful inspection and analysis, that we have, as
a matter of fact, in the case before us, something very much more than a mere repetition
of the same things for the sake of emphasis.
If indeed there were in this instance, mere
reiteration on the part of St. Paul, in important speeches, of a previous narrative of a
most momentous event, we should have no
ground for feeling difficulty or for casting
any imputation upon the authenticity of the
Acts of the Apostles. But, in truth, there is
much more than reiteration in this case   The
same story is indeed told more than once; but
it is so re-told as to have in the re-telling a
distinct relation with both the speaker and
the audience.

The attention which we have given to the
three accounts of St. Paul's Conversion has in

some degree invaded the ground of the proper subject of this lecture, which is the comparison of the Acts with the Epistles, so as to mark their independence of one another and their consistency with one another, and hence the confirmation which each derives from the other We have however been strictly within the range of the *method* of the "Horæ Paulinæ" And, after all, to attempt to put forth any thing like the full details of this comparison, would be to repeat the "Horæ Paulinæ" or to give their substance in another form To do the first would be impossible: and as to the second course, the form of Paley's presentation of his subject could not possibly be improved. It seems best to limit ourselves to some general thoughts which arise on a comparison of the Acts with the Epistles, taking the details of the question for granted. It may be hoped that most of those who read these pages are well acquainted with the book to which I have made such frequent allusion.

As to the action and reaction of the Acts

and Epistles on one another, and the mutual confidence, so to speak, which results from this action and reaction, note how two great subjects, which have been before our attention, in the last lecture and in this, appear consistently in each   These subjects are *the Resurrection of Christ* and the *Conversion of St. Paul*

As regards the former subject, the broad fact is obvious that what is conspicuous in the one section of the New Testament is conspicuous in the other, and that the same feeling in reference to it is manifested in both. Throughout the Acts and the Epistles alike faith in the Resurrection of Christ is an ever-present practical force   It was remarked how the testimony borne to the Resurrection and the manner of bearing that testimony, both by St Paul and by St. Peter, constitute an indissoluble bond between the Acts and the Gospels   But the same testimony of these two Apostles moves on, with the same vehement power and life, *through the Acts into the Epistles.*   I need only refer to the opening of

the Epistle to the Romans—"Jesus Christ
our Lord, declared to be the Son of God with
power, according to the Spirit of holiness, by
the Resurrection from the dead,"—and to the
opening of the first Epistle of Peter—"Blessed
be the God and Father of our Lord Jesus
Christ, which according to His abundant mercy
hath begotten us again unto a lively hope by
the Resurrection of Jesus Christ from the dead."
And these are only specimens. Whatever argument, as regards the unity of Scripture, is
derivable from the witness of these two Apostles to the Resurrection in the Acts, is very
much augmented in strength, when we observe that the witness, in force and in character, is precisely the same in the Epistles
The cord is "threefold," and "cannot easily
be broken"

And next, as regards St Paul's perpetual
recollection of his Conversion, we have been
discussing the question of reiteration—and so
far he does reiterate, that he evidently desires to
express in the most emphatic manner the fact
and the significance of this great change   Just

as he chose it for his main topic in addressing the mob in the Temple Court and in pleading his Master's cause before Festus and Agrippa, so is it when he writes to the Corinthians—"I am not meet to be called an Apostle, because I persecuted the Church of God· but by the grace of God I am what I am"—and when he writes to Timothy—"A blasphemer before, a persecutor and injurious, I obtained mercy . .   for this cause I obtained mercy, that in me first Jesus Christ might show forth all long-suffering" The remembrance of this great change vibrates through St Paul's Epistles, as through all the latter part of the Acts   In both we feel that we have the living personality of the man and the intensity of an ever-present conviction to bind them for us together.

Another general remark which arises out of a comparison of the Acts and the Epistles is this, that *the same character of the Apostle Paul* comes to view on an examination of both   The proofs may be somewhat delicate and minute, but they are very conclusive.

To scatter the names of persons and places
at random over a forged history or over
forged letters, would be a very hazardous
proceeding· for detection would be almost
sure to result on comparison But to exhibit *character* is more hazardous still, unless
there be truth in both the history and the
letters Character reveals itself in small incidents and indirect notices Of course character, and the indications of character, can
be invented, as we see in every book of fiction But this, I think, must be admitted by
all, that the writer of the Acts does not set
himself deliberately to the task of describing
the mental and moral features of St Paul,
and that St Paul's purpose in his Epistles is
not to give a picture of himself In each case
whatever comes to view in this way must come
to view without design.

The discussion which has preceded, concerning the three accounts of St. Paul's Conversion, sets clearly before us that he was a man
of fine tact and great versatility; and this
point might be illustrated by various pas-

sages in his letters. But I select another
aspect of character for our present purpose
Let us take *his sympathetic nature* under consideration and see how it manifests itself alike
in the history and in the letters.

This quality of sympathy is perhaps best
shown in small matters, and very particularly
when small matters are in close contact with
great   "Use a little wine for thy stomach's
sake and thine often infirmities" To write this
in the midst of injunctions on lofty religious
subjects would be natural to some men and
not to others. It was evidently natural to St.
Paul We observe precisely the same feeling
and the same combination in the Epistle to
the Philippians, where reference is made to the
health of Epaphroditus. "Indeed he was sick,
nigh unto death: but God had mercy on him;
and not on him only, but on me also, lest I
should have sorrow upon sorrow:" and presently he adds, "Receive him in the Lord with
all gladness; and hold such in reputation because for the work of the Lord he was nigh
unto death" Something of the same kind is

observed in the shipwreck. During the height of the storm he had said these noble words: "There stood by me this night the angel of God, whose I am and whom I serve, saying, Fear not, Paul; . . . lo, God hath given thee all them that sail with thee." and now, when immediate steps are to be taken for getting safe to land, he says, "This is the fourteenth day that ye have tarried and continued fasting, having taken nothing: wherefore I pray you to take some meat, for this is for your health: for there shall not a hair fall from the head of any of you." To take another instance, what a kindly human sympathy he shows with the Lystrians, when he tells them how "God gave them rain from heaven, and fruitful seasons, filling their heart with food and gladness!" By no mark, perhaps, is a sympathetic nature more surely revealed than in an earnest craving for the sympathy of others. This too is conspicuous in St Paul, and conspicuous everywhere. At Troas "he had no rest in his spirit, because he found not Titus his brother" At Appii

Forum and the Three Taverns, "when he
saw the brethren, he thanked God and took
courage " The former of these sentences is in
an Epistle, the latter is in the Acts He is
constantly referring to his own sufferings It
was *"because of sickness,"* he tells the Galatians, that he staid among them at the first.
He reminds the Macedonians that they knew
how he had been "*shamefully treated*" at
Philippi He reminds the Ephesian elders,
in the speech of Miletus, how from the day
that he came into "Asia," he had been among
them at all seasons "serving the Lord with
all humility of mind, and with *many tears* "
The tone of this speech is in strict harmony
with the Epistles, in most of which, as Paley
has justly remarked, in closing his observa-
tions on the Epistle to Philemon, are "such
pathetic effusions, drawn, for the most part,
from his own sufferings and situation "

This close yet delicate correspondence (and,
let me add, undesigned correspondence) between the Acts and Epistles, in the matter of
St. Paul's character, might be traced in other

particulars and I will ask attention to two of them, before I turn to a topic of a different kind These are St. Paul's *strict consci-entiousness* and his *unswerving tenacity of purpose* They exhibit to us the sterner sides of that varied personality which in its many aspects, yet with strict consistency, is set before us alike in the Acts and the Epistles

Speaking before Felix St. Paul says· "Herein do I exercise myself, to have always a conscience void of offence toward God and toward men" This is a strong statement Alike toward God and toward men he says he had striven to do his duty· and the addition of the word "always" is very characteristic of his style He says too that he made this a matter of self-discipline, of systematic training. He uses here a metaphor from the Greek games. With this should be compared what he says before the Sanhedrim, "Brethren, I have lived in all good conscience before God until this day," and what he says to Festus, "I thought I ought to do many things contrary to the name of Jesus of Nazareth."

And now, if we turn to the Epistles, we find him saying to Timothy, "I thank God, whom I serve from my forefathers with pure conscience," and saying to the Corinthians, "My rejoicing is this, the testimony of my conscience, that in simplicity and godly sincerity I have my conversation in the world" —and again, "I know nothing against myself— nothing is on my conscience—". for this would be a most correct rendering of the passage. And all this is illustrated, not only by his frequent injunctions to the sedulous care of conscience, but by his own sensitive honor with regard to money matters. "I have coveted no man's silver or gold" This he says in his speech to the elders of Ephesus. "If he hath wronged thee, or oweth thee ought, put that on my account: I, Paul, give thee a written promise with my own hand: I will repay thee" This he says in the letter to Philemon —And these are only instances of the proofs of St Paul's strict sense of honor and duty, which could easily be multiplied.

That tenacity of purpose, for which he is em-

inently conspicuous, strikes us the more forc-
ibly, when placed side by side with the sympathy and tenderness, of which I have spoken
above Again to begin with instances from
the Acts, I take simply two from the return-
journey at the close of the Third Missionary
Expedition The scene of one is at Miletus, of
the other at Cæsarea. On the former occasion
he anticipates danger and difficulty: a cloud
of sad foreboding is on his spirit; but he says:
"None of these things move me, neither count
I my life dear unto myself, so that I might finish my course with joy and the ministry which
I have received of the Lord Jesus" On the
second occasion, when he was earnestly "besought not to go up to Jerusalem in the face
of clearly-predicted dangers, "then Paul answered, What mean ye to weep and to break
mine heart? for I am ready not to be bound
only, but also to die at Jerusalem for the
name of the Lord Jesus" The possession of
mere physical courage is not here in question.
It may very rightly be left undecided whether
St. Paul did possess this quality. We have

before our attention a much higher quality of
mind and heart. It is the rising above dis-
couragement, the persevering in spite of difficulty, which constitutes St Paul so noble
an example of tenacity of purpose In the
passages to which reference has been made,
especially when they are taken in combination
with the contemporary Epistles, there is abundant proof of depression of spirits But this
depression did not hinder the most determined perseverance And what we see here
we see everywhere throughout the record of
St Paul in the Acts If he is struck down
by stoning at Lystra, he immediately re-
sumes work elsewhere. If difficult questions
arise at Antioch, he goes up to Jerusalem,
that they be thoroughly discussed. If he is
hindered from preaching the Gospel in Bithynia, he proceeds into Europe. There,
when persecuted at Thessalonica, he moves
on to Berea. He never rests. He is ever
entering upon new ground, ever cheerfully un-
dertaking one task after another, while ever
devoted to one purpose. And is not this

manifestly the same man whom we see in the Epistles? His very style shows the identity of the man There is no need for quoting illustrative instances in detail: and we must now pass to other topics I will only add, while passing from the present topic, that this identity of *character* in the two sections of the New Testament which relate to St. Paul will bear a very close scrutiny, and that this fact, considered as a testimony of truthfulness has very great argumentative force.

I turn now to another general remark, arising out of a comparison of the Acts with the Epistles of St. Paul to the Corinthians, to the Galatians and the Romans. These four Epistles are, even by the most destructive critics, viewed as undoubtedly St Paul's Let us consider what this means This concession is really momentous, both in itself and in the results which logically follow from it. *In these four Epistles we have Christianity.* This would of course be a very scanty Bible, compared with that which we have the happiness of possessing Still we have here the assertion of a Divine revelation, with copious instructions regarding both doctrine and practice But now from this point we can logically advance further. Having this Christianity, we acquire confidence in God, and we believe that He would not deceive us. This tends to spread a feeling of confidence over the rest of the New Testament. What are the results to which this conviction reasonably leads us?

First it is to be observed that there are other Epistles claiming to be St. Paul's, besides the four. If we take the four as our starting-point, we have at once a good standard for comparison. Looking over these Epistles easily and naturally, what do we find? We find unequivocally the same character of the man: we find also the same doctrine, and not merely the same doctrine, but the same manner of presenting it. I confidently say that the evidence derived from this mere general comparison is so overwhelmingly strong that it outweighs all nibbling objections directed against points of detail. This, however, is an argument altogether irrespective of the Acts of the Apostles

But if we bring the Acts into combination with Epistles, our position becomes immediately firmer and more commanding. A fortress already impregnable receives a still further accession of strength. These four Epistles connect themselves, by most distinct and minute evidence, with the Third Missionary Journey of St Paul, as recorded in the Acts. Three of them were undoubtedly written during that journey, and the fourth almost certainly The circumstances of time and place and person in the letters to the Romans and Corinthians are such as to furnish a proof which is almost mathematical The case of the letter to the Galatians is of a different kind; but, for my own part, I think the evidence in this instance as conclusive as in the others In these documents then we obtain a solid ground under our feet—a central table-land, as it were, from whence we can survey the rest of the Epistles And presently we find *them also* to

be connected by close links with the Acts of
the Apostles Thus we obtain, by this kind
of comparison, the conviction of a concatena-
tion among the different parts of the New
Testament, which leads to results far beyond
the starting-point of the argument A table-
land is not an island. We can pass from it to
connecting ridges We can pursue streams
and survey landscapes, all having an essential
relation to the structure of the ground on
which we are treading. In short, if we possess these four Epistles as undoubtedly St
Paul's, we possess *much more* This conclusion is reached by a comparison of the Epistles generally with one another: but it is
largely aided by bringing together the epistolary writings with St. Luke's history.

And one other thought of the same general
character may conclude this lecture. These
epistolary writings are in relation with various parts of Asia Minor, with Northern
and Southern Greece, and finally with Rome,
the centre of the Empire In them we see
the Gospel on its great missionary progress,

attacking many points in succession and almost simultaneously For example, St. Paul in writing to the Corinthians mentions the plans which he had adopted in Galatia: his Epistle to Colossœ and Philippi are sent nearly at the same time And with this general characteristic of the Paulinæ epistolary writings the Acts are entirely correspondent. The whole air and feeling derivable from the one class of documents is similar to that which we derive from the other. In St Luke's narrative there is all the impression of a world-wide enterprise: and this impression becomes stronger and more life-like at the end. In comparing the Acts with the Gospels, reference was made to the Hebrew back-ground, which was then necessarily present to our thoughts I spoke of the Mount of Olives as one natural place of transition. But the voyage of the Apostle from Cæsarea to Puteoli introduces us to associations of a totally different kind. Not Judæa and the Sea of Galilee are the subjects before us now, but the wide Mediterranean and Europe to the far

west   The mere fact that Cæsarea was on
the sea-coast is a prophecy of the future.
We are vividly conscious of this, whether we
think of St. Peter or of St. Paul in connection with that place.   But with the planting
of St Paul's footsteps upon that mole at
Puteoli, large fragments of which still remain as though in conscious memory of the
fact, a new era for the world began.   Thence-
forward the onward view of Christian missionary hope was without limit   That often-
quoted line, which is now, I believe, inscribed
on the portals of a University on the shores
of the Pacific,

"Westward the course of empire holds its way,"

that famous line receives its highest meaning when it is applied to the progress of the
Gospel: and all this progress is involved in
that voyage which is recorded in the Acts.

I have not thought it necessary to enter
upon any disquisitions regarding the precise
plan and purpose of the Acts of the Apostles; the reasons why its particular form was

given to it and its particular limitations imposed upon it. Two things indeed are very clear, first that whereas St. Luke's former treatise describes the Lord's working on earth, this reveals to us His manner of working from heaven, and secondly that only select specimens of this working are given to us in the Acts, the greater part being left in obscurity. But I may end here with a phrase which is really full of meaning, though it can hardly be accepted, as it has sometimes been proposed, for a complete definition of the purpose of the book. The phrase, to which I refer, is simply this—"from Jerusalem to Rome." That sentence of St Paul carried with it the best hopes of future times and of Western lands, when he said, in the midst of his Third Missionary Journey—"After I have been at Jerusalem, I must also see Rome."

LECTURE IV.

THE USEFULNESS OF THE BOOK FOR INSTRUCTION AND EDIFICATION.

LECTURE IV.

*THE USEFULNESS OF THE BOOK FOR INSTRUC-
TION AND EDIFICATION*

HAVING now looked back, so to speak, from the Central Table Land of the Acts of the Apostles, so as to trace the connection of this book with the Gospels, and having looked forward from it along the line of the Associated Epistles, we may now in this last lecture revert to such general views of the value of the book, as occupied our attention in the first lecture—with this difference, however, that then we 'considered certain features of it, which commended it, almost at first sight, as a Divine gift, infinitely worthy of our thankful acceptance,— whereas now we are to examine closely the benefits which the Church derives from it in useful instruction and spiritual edification.

And first, I suggest that we take notice of its *connection with history*, its exact yet unpremeditated correspondence with the real facts of the case, as regards events and persons and places, in the time to which its narrative belongs I am disposed to lay very much stress upon this characteristic of the book as a ground for our confidence. I think I have observed that very scanty attention is paid to this kind of evidence, when an endeavor is made to show that this document is a comparatively late composition, to be almost classed with the Apocryphal Acts. But such evidence is really an argument of the utmost force, especially when we take account not only of the historical details with which we come in contact in this book, but of the manner of this contact. For the manner shows that the writer was contemporary with the circumstances which he happens to mention. He not only relates the history, but he personally touched it.

It has been said by the present Bishop of Durham that "no ancient work affords so

many tests of veracity, for no other has such
numerous points of contact in all directions
with contemporary history, politics, and ty-
pography, whether Jewish or Greek or Roman" This is a strong statement, but it is
no exaggeration; and it is important that we
should mark it; for every one of these points
of contact is a point of danger, unless there
is very exact truthfulness and an easy naturalness in the mode of their appearance. Of
course this aspect of the matter before us
must be illustrated by a selection of examples; and the selected examples cannot be numerous. I will slightly notice, in the first instance, four places and four persons; the places
shall be Thessalonica and Ephesus, Lasæa
and Phœnix The persons shall be Gamaliel,
Herod Agrippa I., Gallio, and Bernice As
regards the first two places, let it be observed that political geography, if it is true
to the facts of the period, is a decisive corroboration of political history. The second
two places are examples of very recent confirmation by discovery As respects the per-

sons I have named, it will be noted that
one is strictly Jewish, another strictly Imperial and Roman, while the two others are
members of the Herodian family. In the Acts
of the Apostles we are on the line of inter-
section between Jewish history and Roman
history: and on that line the Herodian family occupy a position of extraordinary interest.

In St. Luke's notice of Thessalonica there
is an incidental confirmatory fact so remarkable that it is almost startling; and I have
often wondered that more heed has not been
given to it In describing the tumult caused
there by the Jews in the matter of Paul and
Silas, the historian uses (quite naturally, and
without raising any question) a very strange
word for those who appear in our Authorized
Version as the "rulers of the city." The
word is *politarchs*. It is not found in any
ancient writer. But travellers within the present century have seen and read this word
politarchs conspicuously cut on stone in ancient inscriptions among the surviving remains
of the place. No evidence could possibly be

stronger; and the peculiarity of the word enhances its value

As regards the second city named above,
Bishop Lightfoot remarks again, "We are
justified in saying that ancient literature has
preserved no picture of the Ephesus of Imperial times comparable for its life-like truthfulness to the narrative of St Paul's sojourn
there in the Acts" Two features of the
case which come forth to view on an examination of a profuse number of inscriptions
recently discovered and arranged, are that
the worship of "the Great Goddess Diana"
was the predominant enthusiasm of the place,
and that "the Theatre," under the open sky,
was the customary centre of excited popular
crowds. These inscriptions too (illustrated by
abundant coins) set before us, in remarkable
combination, the title of the "Town Clerk,"
the mention of the "lawful assembly," the
"chief of Asia," or the Asiarchs who pre-
sided over the games, and the fact that the
province of "Asia" was governed by "dep-
uties" or proconsuls. That remarkable word

too, *neocoros*, rendered "worshipper" in the English version, but more correctly translated "temple-warden" or "temple-sweeper," in which Ephesus gloried, comes conspicuously before our eyes in these ancient, yet fresh and eloquent, testimonies Even emperors boasted that they were (to use an equivalent translation) "sacristans" of the famous local Divinity

I now come to the mention of Lasæa It will be remembered that the naming of this place occurs quite casually, so to speak, in the Acts of the Apostles Under stress of weather, in the course of the voyage towards Rome, the Alexandrian cornship, which had the Apostle on board, came into the roadstead of Fair Havens, "nigh whereunto was the city of Lasæa" St Luke was probably conscious of no special reason for mentioning the place. It may be presumed that the town attracted the attention of the passengers as the ship entered the roadstead, and that intercourse with it was frequent afterwards through the bringing of supplies to the people on board Thus the naming of Lasæa became a natural part of the historian's description Certainly he did not deposit this local name in his narrative as a riddle to be solved after many centuries by a party of Scotch travellers The point of interest is that while Fair Havens is perfectly well known and has always retained the same designation, Lasæa was never till lately identified, except by very precarious conjecture, not to speak of tampering with Greek manuscripts, for the sake of procuring identification A quick eye, from the deck of a yacht, some twenty-five years ago, discerned some ruins in precisely the right spot, and on landing, a question asked from a shepherd obtained the immediate answer, " The place is called Lasæa "

With the identification of Phœnix I can connect, if I may be allowed to say so, almost a personal interest. It is at the moment of leaving Fair Havens for the westward that this harbor of Phœnix is named in St Luke's narrative. It might be said on a superficial view that we have really no concern with this harbor, since the place was never really reached   But clearly there was such a harbor to the west of Fair Havens   The sailors knew it well, and they described it as sheltered from north-west and south-west winds. The question is whether there is any such anchorage, in the right place, which satisfies these conditions   For a long period it was asserted that no such anchorage was known there   I have myself received a negative reply, on putting the inquiry before one well acquainted with the south coast of Crete   But on the arrival at the English Admiralty of the drawings executed by the surveying officers, I found at once what I was sure would be proved to exist. I had the satisfaction of first publishing the information that there is here a safe harbor, with deep water, precisely sheltered from the above named winds, and with the name *Phineka* close by, and thus the discovery of this place is to be added to those geographical evidences of the truth of the Bible, which have been accumulating plentifully during recent years.

From places let us now pass to persons. There are in the Acts of the Apostles two notices of Gamaliel, quite independent of one another, quite consistent with one another, but evidently not made of set purpose to correspond, and in each case arising quite naturally out of the narrative His wise counsel is named in an early chapter, during the discussions on the apprehension of Peter and the other Apostles for teaching heresy In a later chapter, when St. Paul is giving an account of his early days at Jerusalem, he states that this same man was his instructor in Theology. Now the great Rabbi Gamaliel is a well-known personage in the Talmudical annals of the time The chronology agrees with what we read in the Acts, and it is equally important to add that the character of Gamaliel agrees with what we read there: for he was not only a Pharisee, but a man of candor and liberal thought, and much opposed to the bigotry of a well-known rival school. Thus our book is found to connect itself in an easy and unpremeditated manner with the life

10

of one who has been justly termed "a hero of Rabbinic history"

And if Gamaliel correctly links this book with Rabbinic history so does King Herod Agrippa I link it, in exact particulars, with the Greek-writing Jewish annalist Josephus Agrippa's desire to "please the Jews" is equally manifest in both authorities. The accounts of his death at Cæsarea agree in various details—in the pompous display, in the brilliant garments, in the "set day," in the nature of the sudden and fatal disease, while there are differences in the manner of relating the story, which absolutely preclude the possibility of any copying. Moreover the dates are in harmony, so that in fact the death of Herod Agrippa in the year 44 becomes one of the pivots, which help us in arranging correctly the chronology of the Acts of the Apostles.

The name of Gallio supplies to us a link with general Roman history of a totally different kind The title given to this governor of Achaia is correct: for at that moment it was a proconsular province, whereas at a date very slightly different this would not have been the case Gallio was the brother of Seneca, and has a conspicuous place in that philosopher's letters, besides being known to us through other writers In this literature he is distinctly connected with the province of Achaia; and moreover his character is described to us as amiable and easy, such as would readily allow any difficult questions to pass by. This is in harmony with all that we read of what took place at Corinth in the course of St Paul's Second Missionary Journey. The narrative too has all the air of a contemporary account, without any trace of the exercise of ingenuity, and is very unlike a part of a romance constructed, a century later, for a polemical purpose

With Bernice we return to the Herodian family, but in a later generation than that to which the former reference belonged She was the daughter of the first Herod Agrippa, and the sister of the second, in whose com-

pany she is presented to us by the writer of
the Acts The scene comes at once very
vividly into our memory, and we mark not
only the pomp and parade with which she
and Agrippa came with Festus into the
audience hall, to hear the prisoner Paul,
but also the fact that when this brilliant
company swept out of the chamber, Bernice
is again named, as though she were the
most noteworthy of all then present. If from
this we look into contemporary history, it is
startling to observe how she appears there.
It was an age of profligate women: and
among such women the Herodian Bernice
was notorious through the empire It is not
pleasant to write of such a subject. Her life
reads, as has been truly said, "like a horri-
ble romance." But it is of high importance
to note that what we find in this passage of
the Acts of the Apostles is in harmony with
what we learn from historians and satirists,
even to the jewellery which Agrippa gave
to this shameless woman.

These instances have been very lightly

touched: and in them the list of available instances has been by no means exhausted. Other places and other persons might have been brought forward from the pages of the Acts of the Apostles with similar results. and the temptation to linger upon this part of the subject is so great, that I will ask you to think, in this connection, of yet one more place and one more person The place shall be Cyprus and the person Felix

There are recent circumstances, both in your country and ours, which give a special animation and interest to the mention of Cyprus Whatever may be the import and result of the English occupation of Cyprus, this occupation is by no means a common-place fact. Nor is it a common-place fact that General de Cesnola has brought to the New World very ancient and very precious memorials of the religious worship of that island. But in the midst of these topics of conversation I wonder whether it has ever occurred to my hearers that this island is named on eight distinct occasions in the Acts

of the Apostles, and in each case in such a
manner as to suggest very useful instruction.
We are here concerned chiefly with the evidential aspect of these passages   I will name
simply three points of view from which we
should regard them   First, there is the strict
geographical accuracy with which the island
comes before us in all these varied and incidental notices   Thus it is conspicuously
in sight from the coast near Antioch, and
it was naturally first visited on the earliest
missionary expedition   again its high ground
was sighted on the voyage from Rhodes to
Tyre, at the close of the Third Missionary
Expedition, and this is a touch in the narrative which could only arise from truth; and,
once more, the sailing under the lee of Cyprus, "because the winds were contrary," is
one of the most life-like details of the early
part of that voyage to Italy, during which
the narrator was St. Paul's companion   Secondly, we know from good authority that at
this period the Jews were numerous in Cyprus   (For instance Herod the Great farmed

copper-mines in the island) This fact is well illustrated for us by what we are told in the Acts concerning Barnabas, by what is said of Cypriot Missionaries in the account of the first spread of the Gospel beyond the limits of Palestine, and by the fact that there were more synagogues than one at Salamis, the first city evangelized on the first general mission. Thirdly, the political designation of Sergius Paulus is in exact correspondence with the circumstances of the time, and has recently received an unexpected confirmation. It has been long known that Cyprus was at this time, like Asia and Achaia, a proconsular province, though earlier commentators thought it was still, as it had been a short time before, an imperial province, so that St Luke may be said to have narrowly escaped an historical error. But, moreover, one of the inscriptions so carefully given in Cesnola's *Cyprus*, is one in which we read the words, "in the proconsulate of Paulus," There seems no reason for doubting that this is the identical Sergius Paulus of the Acts;

and this circumstance arrests our attention the more, because we are here at the transition-point of the Apostle's own change of name

The presence of Felix in the history of the Acts of the Apostles should be carefully noted: for his giving place to Festus in the governorship of the province, in the year 60, furnishes us with our second pivot for adjusting the chronology of the book   But this is by no means the whole of what requires our attention in connection with Felix   The complexion of the social and moral state of the province,.as indicated by the sacred historian, corresponds with what we learn from other sources of the utterly corrupt condition of the priestly party at Jerusalem, and the presence of banditti and assassins in the country.   Nor must we omit to mark the character of Felix himself.   He was mean, corrupt, and oppressive.   He had once been a slave; and he was raised by court favor to his high position, in which, to use the strong expression of the great Latin annalist, he * " exercised the power of a king with the

temper of a slave " We thoroughly understand what is said by St. Luke of his hope
"that money should have been given him of
Paul, " and the circumstances under which he
was recalled from his province by Nero afford a
very good reason for his "wishing to show the
Jews a pleasure" with regard to this prisoner.
Drusilla was with him when he visited St. Paul
in prison; and his marriage with this sister of
Bernice is one of the well-known facts of con-
temporaneous history. There is no stranger
event than the death of Drusilla, with the
child she bore to Felix, in the eruption of
Vesuvius near to the place where St. Paul
landed on his arrival in Italy.

In these notices of Cyprus and of Felix, the
earlier and later parts of the Apostle's voyage
have been lightly touched, and it is proper to
add that the particulars of that voyage furnish
to us some of the most important evidences of
truthfulness under this general head of historical accuracy. These, however, must be left
on one side I will simply content myself
with one quotation confirmatory of what we

are told concerning the shipwreck on the coast
of Malta—a quotation all the more valuable,
because it comes from a civilian, who recently
held high office under the English Govern-
ment   The name of Sir William Reid is well
known in connection with "The Law of
Storms," and Mr. Hermann Merivale says,
in his account of a visit to Malta·—"Sir
William Reid was a great reader of Scripture,
and as some veterans are said to be specially
partial to the warlike books of Joshua and
Kings, so he, for his part, had certainly a pre-
dilection for those chapters which contain the
narrative of St Paul's tempestuous voyage.
The first place he took me to in Malta was
the well-known little bay, or rather creek,
known by the name of the Saint.   Under
such guidance as his, the absolute and un-
mistakable identity of the spot with that described in the Acts flashed irresistibly upon the
mind, and all sceptical notions about an Adri-
atic 'Melita' were dispelled at once.   There
was the very point on which a vessel, driven
along the northern side of the island by stress

of Euroclydon, and finding the precise soundings specified in the narrative, would naturally be driven   There was the 'creek with a shore,' almost the only beach of sand on that rocky line of coast   There was the 'place where two seas,' caused by the protrusion of an insulated rock just in the entrance of the bay, 'meet' close to the 'shore' aforesaid Under his description, every incident of the tale seemed as if enacted before the eye   We scarcely needed, to excite our imaginations, the singular experience which befell a friend of mine at this spot, where a serpent dropt from a fagot of brushwood, which he had casually taken up " To what is here quoted regarding one single part of that varied narrative of the Voyage and Shipwreck, I will only add this remark, that just as every part of it can be illustrated from classical writers, so does this narrative give us fuller information as to the ships and navigation of classical times than any single document that has come down to us from antiquity

Passing from this view of the subject, our

minds are led by an easy transition to set
a high value on this Book of the Acts *in its
use for purposes of education.* It follows from
what has been said above that its educational
usefulness must be very great, both because
the book itself is a part of general history,
and because it brings the origin of the Church
into the easiest combination with historical instruction. It may safely be predicted that
whatever changes, social or national, take
place in the theory or practice of education,
the Greek language will ever hold its ground
in the higher linguistic teaching, and that the
annals of the Roman Empire will ever be the
magnificent background of historical teaching   Attempts will be made from time to
time, and justifiable and successful attempts,
to assert for other things a high place in edu-
cating mankind : but the power of the Greek
language over the human mind will revive
again and again and will survive : so too it
will be felt that there is a greatness in the
Roman Empire which belongs to no other
historical subject, at least until what is now

the future becomes the past With these two thoughts in the mind we see the fruitful value of the Acts of the Apostles for higher education It has placed the origin of the Christian Church, within the high sphere of the Greek language, in dignified connection with Roman history, and herein we are bound to see and adore the traces of Divine providence.

But for elementary schools likewise this Book of the Acts has the utmost value. If the young and the ignorant are to obtain some intelligent notions of classical antiquity, of the spread of the Greek language, of the institutions of the Roman Empire, there is no better method than in the use of this book ; while certainly it is an advantage that such subjects should be approached in so religious and healthy an atmosphere Then let us call to mind the diversified interest of the book —its perpetual variety of incident and place and character—its alternations of narratives and speeches—its capability too of illustration by maps and charts and coins, and by views of 'existing remains, from the great stones of the substructions of the Temple-area at Jerusalem, above which Solomon's Porch once stood, to the glory which still crowns the ruins of the Acropolis at Athens, and finally to the fragments of the pavement of the Appian Way, upon which St Paul's feet undoubtedly trod when his long adventurous voyage was over

One of the most curious parts of this subject is the contact of the History of the Apostles with Heathen Mythology. On two occasions, and in each case quite naturally, and in a manner very unlike any thought that would have occurred to an ingenious controversial composer after the event, Greek and Roman divinities come before us in the narrative   It was a common belief that Jupiter and Mercury were in the habit of visiting the earth in companionship; and Ovid localizes an occasion of this kind in the very neighborhood of Lycaonia. Nothing then could be more true to the nature of the case, than when we find the poor untutored heathens of this region rushing to the conclusion that they

were so visited again, as their forefathers had
been, when Paul and Barnabas came among
them . and an additional touch of reality is
given to the story, when we read that they
identified Paul with Mercury, "because he was
the chief speaker," while, if they saw something majestic and benignant in the aspect
of Barnabas, this is quite in harmony with
what we know of his character   And the other instance arises out of the narrative quite as
simply and unaffectedly, though in a manner
quite different   Just as Luke and his companions observed on entering Fair Havens the
proximity of the town of Lasæa, so, when they
left Malta for Rome, and were taken on board
another great Alexandrian cornship, they could
not fail to have their attention called to the
fact that her name was the "Castor and Pol-
lux." The figures of those "great twin brethren," the recognized patrons of Greek and Roman sailors, were conspicuously before their
eyes, as they prepared to go on deck. It has
pleased God that such features should be characteristic of the Acts, and we ought to be by

no means reluctant to acknowledge them and to feel their value, when we address ourselves to the instruction of the ignorant and young.

I have been led to take a profound interest in the Sunday-school work of this country; and all the more because in England we are about to hold a centenary celebration of the beginning of an institution full of blessing to all who speak our native tongue, and I am thankful to know that this Book of the Acts, on either side of the Atlantic, can be made charming and instructive by painstaking Sunday-school teachers to multitudes of those who will manage the world in years to come.

Next let us regard this book *as a Missionary Manual.* This is an aspect of its usefulness, upon which the highest value is to be set; for Mission-work is the active life of the Church. This again is a view of our subject to which there will be an immediate response in America. One of the happy bonds between your country and ours, and of the cheerful hopes for the future of the world, resides in this fact, that in both countries during the

last fifty years there has been great Missionary
activity. Speaking indeed on this subject here,
I must think of names of great men, not be-
longing to our communion, such as Brainerd
and Eliot. But that which was specially in
my mind was what I observed at the General Convention at Baltimore in 1871, and
what was doubtless equally conspicuous at
New York and Boston in 1874 and 1877, the
reports of Missionary effort and success in
various parts of the world, which were made
day by day. A Church, in which there is
this living interest in the progress of the
Gospel, must necessarily be strong.

There can be no mistake as to the Missionary spirit which pervades the Acts of the
Apostles. The whole temper of the book is
aggressive, beneficently aggressive. Even like
the sunrise in the morning it insists on perpetual advance. The book means nothing at
all, if it does not mean this. It is no mere
record of an interesting phase of religious
thought, or of the useful consequences of a
benevolent life; but it is charged with a power

11

which is to affect the world, and to move on through all future ages, and never be arrested till limits are discovered to time and space Moreover, it asserts most distinctly, though in no unsympathetic and harsh spirit, that Christianity is not one only of many religions possessing equal claims, but it is *the one* religion destined to supersede the rest. From this source then we can draw, ever fresh and vigorous, that Missionary enthusiasm, which is the strength of the Church and the hope of mankind.

Not only, however, the spirit of Missionary work, but the right *methods* of Missionary work are presented to us in this book: and I will now venture on stating a few of those principles of Christian Missions, which come to view on a careful study of the Acts of the Apostles, and which ought to receive attention, because they are of binding force for all time.

First mark that the progress of the Gospel is made to depend on *personal effort*. Living religion in the heart of one man kindles living religion in the heart of other men "The man of Ethiopia," in returning from Jerusalem along the "desert" road near Gaza, and "seated in his chariot," is reading "the prophet Esaias"; and it is said from heaven to Philip "Go near and join thyself to this chariot" The consequence was that the "Ethiopian went on his way rejoicing"; and what results followed as to Christianity in Africa we cannot calculate. Apollos, when his spirit had been quickened, and his mind instructed by Aquila and Priscilla, passed over from Ephesus to Achaia, and "there helped them much which had believed through grace" Under the same head of personal exertion must be classed all that we read concerning St Peter in the early part of the Acts, and the progressive spread of the Gospel, along the narrow coast-region of Judæa, and in the later part concerning St. Paul and the great expeditions which connect his name with Thessalonica, Ephesus, Corinth, and Rome.

Still we should observe, in the second place, that this missionary effort is not detached effort. On the contrary, *co-operation* is a most distinct feature of the labor on behalf of the Gospel described in the Acts of the Apostles Peter and John are sent *together* to Samaria. Barnabas takes a journey to Tarsus to fetch Paul to Antioch. On the First Missionary Expedition they go together to Cyprus, and John Mark with them. On the Second Missionary Expedition, after there has been a dispute and separation, Paul takes Silas with him into the interior of Asia Minor, and, finding Timothy there, him also "would he have to go forth with him" On the Third Expedition he is at Ephesus, and purposes to go onward to Macedonia. "*So*," it is said, "he sent into Macedonia," to precede him, "two of them that ministered unto him, Timotheus and Erastus." We know, of course, that if we were to allow ourselves to wander into the region of the Epistles, this great principle and method could be illustrated profusely from thence.

Another point to be carefully observed in the history of Mission-work, as related in the

Acts, is that the Gospel spreads by the use of *the living voice* "Faith cometh by hearing; and hearing by the Word of God" This great principle is illustrated in the recorded history, alike of St Peter and St Paul It is probable indeed that, as a preacher, the former was far greater than the latter. Our overlooking of this fact is perhaps part of that injustice towards St Peter, of which I spoke in a former lecture Certainly the effect of his sermons, in the multitude of conversions which followed, is such as we do not see elsewhere. But in the life of the other Apostle, on the most varied occasions, at Antioch in Pisidia, on the Areopagus at Athens, in the audience chamber at Cæsarea, the same great principle, enunciated by himself, is abundantly exemplified

At the same time another conspicuous fact of missionary experience, as set before us in the Acts, is to be carefully combined with that which has just been named This is the appointed preparation for success in the wide diffusion of the Greek Translation of the

Ancient Scriptures "Moses of old time hath
in every city them that preach him, being
read in the synagogues every Sabbath Day"
I will quote here some words used by the
present Bishop of Lincoln in his Introduction
to the Acts of the Apostles. Through the
Septuagint Version, he says, "Even Hea-
thenism itself had been silently leavened by
the diffusion of the Hebrew Scriptures Their
venerable antiquity, their noble simplicity,
their pure morality, had won for them the
affections of many wise and noble minds,
which were wearied and disgusted with the
jarring contradictions and the licentious prof-
ligacy of Paganism, and recognized in the
religion of the Old Testament a divine echo
responsive to the voices of Nature, Reason,
and Conscience speaking in their own hearts."
Is it not evident that the same principle of
preparatory mission-work is applicable to the
diffusion of the *New Testament* among Heathen nations now, and that results in the
Far East through Christian literature may
reasonably be expected, corresponding with

what we find to have taken place of old in connection with the synagogues of the dispersed Jews ?

Another great feature of early Missionary work, especially as regards St Paul, is to be found in the fact that he always *aimed at great cities*. The period in which he lived was an age of great cities   The place where the Christian Church first received its distinctive name, and where the first great success was achieved outside Judæa, was Antioch, which ranked third among the cities of the Empire   On the shores of the Ægean were three great mercantile emporiums.   On the Second Missionary Journey the prolonged residences, of which we have a careful account, were at two of them—Thessalonica and Corinth.   It was doubtless the wish to work for Christ in Ephesus, the third, which made St Paul desire " to preach the Gospel in Asia "   On the Last Missionary Journey the wish was at length fulfilled.   Finally we see how the yearning of his heart tended towards Rome, and how some of the most signal benefits which he rendered to the world were done in that metropolis, partly though the Epistle to Rome, partly through the Epistles written from thence   And once more is there not a close parallel here with our own times ? We, too, live in an age of great cities.   Our part is boldly to imitate the Apostolic example.   Such places as New York, Chicago, and San Francisco, are the colossal modern counterparts of the cities of the Roman Empire.

One other particular may close this enumeration of Missionary principles, as presented to us in the Book of the Acts.   St. Paul was careful to establish a local fixed ministry in every spot where the Gospel had been planted. At the close of the First Journey, when they were preparing to return to Antioch, and were revisiting their old ground, "they ordained them elders in every city."   A clear proof of the same habit of procedure is to be seen in the sending from Miletus to Ephesus and "calling for the elders of the Church"; and long afterwards decisive corroboration of this

practice is found in one of the latest Epistles
" For this cause," he says to Titus, " I left
thee in Crete, that thou shouldest ordain elders in every city "

Very closely connected with this subject
is one which very seriously and happily af-
fects us all, whether we are directly engaged
in Mission-work or not. The Book of the
Acts is a series of *Lessons in Providence.*
How manifestly, in the course of its story,
do we see temporary evils overruled for per-
manent good ! Persecution becomes the opportunity for wider diffusion of the Gospel.
Flagrant sins, as in the case of Ananias and
Sapphira and Simon Magus, result in solemn
admonitions recorded for the benefit of every
age And, to pass that which was more particularly in my thoughts, we see throughout
how the circumstances of life are a discipline
of dependence and an incitement to prayer.

Disengaging the movements of St. Paul
from the question of missionary progress, and
viewing him personally, I think we may regard the circumstances of his life as a prov-

idential training, and as thus furnishing both admonition and encouragement to ourselves. He meets with friends, just when he needs their companionship and assistance, as, for instance, Timotheus at Lystra and Aquila and Priscilla at Corinth He is not permitted to preach the Gospel in the provinces of Asia and Bithynia: but this results in a prosperous entry on the evangelization of Europe. He embarks cheerfully and hopefully on this new enterprise; and presently he is hindered and persecuted On his return to Palestine from his Last Missionary Expedition he is kept two years in prison This is very mysterious We feel as if the world could not spare "two years" from such a life And yet it may be that this discipline was most salutary to himself, as certainly it is very usefully admonitory to us He has long desired to go to Rome. He does go thither: but certainly in a manner most unexpected to himself On his way thither he passes through the utmost danger, and he is shipwrecked. Still his life is saved.

We might pursue this train of thought into many particulars Even the smaller incidents are suggestive Look for instance at that boat which is towing behind, while "the south wind is blowing softly," and the sailors suppose they have "obtained their purpose" of reaching the harbor of Phœnix. They little expected the furious gale, which suddenly drove them out of their course: and under the lee of Clauda "they had much work to come by the boat" Still they did succeed in taking it on board. Finally, after a fortnight, when the ship in the night, on the coast of Malta, depends simply on her four anchors, and is in danger of foundering, the sailors lower the boat and attempt to leave the ship If they had succeeded, all the passengers would have been drowned. But the Apostle had a friend on board, and he acted on the emergency with consummate judgment. "He said to the Centurion and to the soldiers, Except these abide in the ship, ye cannot be saved Then the soldiers cut off the ropes of the boat and let her fall off."

In the end all were saved without the boat. A profitable sermon might be preached on the incidents connected with this boat. They furnish to us a parable of the mysterious providence, under which our human life is spent.

And to revert for a moment to Peter, with the same thought in our minds How remarkably he was guided, in the case of Cornelius, to unexpected results! On the whole, omitting the miraculous (and we must omit the miraculous), we gain from this book instruction in the reality of providential guidance, most comforting, most encouraging for all our doings, and especially for our efforts in religious work.

There is a religious lesson of another kind, which, I think, ought not to be altogether omitted from this brief summary of the advantages derivable from this book. I will venture to term it the lesson of *Judicious Compromise in Religion*, though I am aware that such a phrase might easily be misunderstood I shall best explain what I mean by an enumeration of instances. Peter and

John go to the Temple "at the hour of prayer." They do not break rudely and suddenly with the old institutions of their fathers The Apostles show great frankness in listening to Peter's argument regarding Cornelius, and in accepting the result. "Then hath God unto the Gentiles given repentance unto life." The attitude, again, of James at the Council is full of candor. He accepts well-attested truth and lays aside all prejudice. The utmost consideration and forbearance are observable in the letter issued by the Council, in which rules of diet, for the sake of the Jewish converts and of the Jews, are elevated for the time to the dignity of moral principles. Once more, Paul does not object to bind himself by a Nazaritic vow, or to make common cause with those who are so bound. All these things give to the spirit of the book a decided character of forbearance, which in the midst of ardent missionary zeal, must have largely contributed, under God, to the early success of Christianity, while it is a perpetual example to ourselves.

If our limits of space made it possible, I might have desired to dwell with some care on two features of the Book of the Acts, which certainly fall under the general description of profitable edification and instruction. These are its exhibition of single unceasing devotion to God and to the cause of Christ, and its unity of religious doctrine with that which we find in the other books of the New Testament They are two very different subjects; but each of them is of obvious importance, when this history is treated evidentially.

As to the first point, we have this advantage, that a very few words will suffice to make the fact evident From the beginning to the end of the book we trace, in those who are engaged in founding Christianity, a straightforward, unswerving, onward movement, in obedience to a direct commission; and it is of the greater consequence to mark this, because of what has been said above regarding religious compromise " We cannot but speak the things which we have seen and heard; we ought to obey God rather than men," are the words of Peter and the other Apostles, when confronted by the unbelieving Jews, "and daily in the Temple, and in every house, they ceased not to teach and preach Jesus Christ;" and as with the earlier Apostles, so with St Paul upon a wider field To the elders of Ephesus, while he says, on the one hand, of the past: "I have taught you publicly and from house to house; I have not shunned to declare unto you all the counsel of God, by the space of three years I ceased not to warn every one day and night with tears,"—he says of the future, which to his clear apprehension is full of threatening danger: "None of these things move me, neither count I my life dear unto myself, so that I might finish my course with joy, and the ministry, which I have received of the Lord Jesus" Presently afterwards, landing at Cæsarea, and met by the distinct prophecies of coming evil, he exclaims "What mean ye to weep and to break mine heart? for I am ready, not to be bound only, but

also to die for the Lord Jesus," and to quote
one example more of this unflinching devotion of heart in the Apostle Paul, as set before us in the Acts, it is most striking to
hear in the midst of the storm, when he can
speak only a few words, and when his encouragement to the terrified crew would in
fact have been complete without the paren-
thesis, saying of himself "whose I am and
whom I serve" No sermon was ever so short
or so well fitted to its occasion. It is, however, as a proof of *unflinching devotion* to his
Master, that I here bring forward this most
remarkable utterance

The allusion, too, to the *Doctrine* of the
Acts of the Apostles must be made very
briefly; but a very brief allusion will suffice
to justify what has been said of its consistency with the Doctrine of other parts of
the New Testament Nothing in the teaching of St. Peter or St. Paul, as here recorded,
can be pointed out which is not in harmony
with the teaching of their Epistles. Even
the statement of this fact in its general form

is not without its value in its relation to the trustworthiness of the Acts. But two passages of a decisive character may be adduced with advantage, each connected with a very marked occasion, and each setting forth the doctrine of free justification through faith. St. Peter said at the Apostolic Council, " God put no difference between us and the Gentiles, purifying their hearts by faith. We believe that through the grace of the Lord Jesus Christ we shall be saved even as they " We seem here to have the mature teaching of St. Peter's First Epistle. St. Paul said, in his great sermon at Antioch in Pisidia, " Through this man is preached unto you the forgiveness of sins; and by Him all that believe are justified from all things, from which ye could not be justified by the law of Moses " Have we not here a summary of the whole course of thought in the Epistles to the Romans and the Galatians ?

I have reserved to the last the topic which appears to me of pre-eminent importance The constant mention of the Holy Spirit, the constant recognition of the supremacy of the Holy Spirit, is more characteristic of this book, as regards religious teaching, than anything else. So prominent, so distinguishing a fact is this, that the book has been beautifully and truly termed "the Gospel of the Holy Ghost." The one most remarkable feature in the doctrine of the book is the prominence given in it to the work and offices of the Third Person of the Holy Trinity. The history of the early days of the Christian Church, as told in these Acts, is, so to speak, a specimen of the way in which the Lord Jesus will continue "to do and to teach" from His Royal Throne in Heaven, by the power of the Holy Ghost sent down according to His own solemn words to His disciples the night before the Cross   "If I depart, I will send the Comforter to you. When He is come, He will guide you into all truth."

As to the facts of the case, I believe that a simple condensed enumeration of them will be more forcible than any comment. And this enumeration may be given in two ways.

First, there are the broad general features of the case, the instances where the mention of the Holy Spirit is evidently meant to have a commanding position at critical parts of the narrative But, also, there are many minor examples, if we may so call them, where the same Power is shown to be consciously felt, so that the whole tissue of the narrative is pervaded by this influence In combining these two aspects of the question we perceive how great is the importance which it rightfully assumes

At the beginning of the Acts Whitsuntide breaks on us like a sunrise From the outset everything works rapidly up to this point The Lord, after His resurrection, had, "through the Holy Ghost," given to His Apostles commandments : they were to be "baptized with the Holy Ghost"; to receive power after that the "Holy Ghost had come upon them" Then came Pentecost with all its wonder and efficacy. But, in the next place, there was a second Pentecost, a second Whitsuntide, at Cæsarea, in the case of Cornelius The whole account of his conversion is pervaded by the mention of the Holy Spirit. It was the voice of "the Spirit," as St Luke tells us, and as St Peter relates afterwards, which determined his departure with the messengers While Peter was speaking to Cornelius and his friends, "the Holy Ghost fell on all them which heard the Word," so that those who had come with Peter were astonished, "because that on the Gentiles also was poured the gift of the Holy Ghost." Then follows the question of Peter, "Can any forbid the water, that these should not be baptized, which have received the Holy Ghost as well as we?" And we should mark how he urges this point when he is justifying his conduct before the apostles and brethren. "As I began to speak, the Holy Ghost fell on them, as on us at the beginning: then remembered I the words of the Lord, how that He said, John indeed baptized with water, but ye shall be baptized with the Holy Ghost"—and how He said long afterwards, "Ye know how that a good while ago God made choice among us that the Gentiles by my mouth should hear the word of the Gospel and believe. and God, which knoweth the hearts, bare them witness, giving to them the Holy Ghost, even as He did unto us" And to turn to a third point, which may well be said to be of critical moment, the same power of the Second Person of the Trinity is named as presiding over the earliest formation of the Christian Ministry. The Seven Deacons chosen to assist the Apostles are, by authority, selected as "men full of the Holy Ghost"; and Stephen, the most prominent of the seven, is especially named as "full of the Holy Ghost," while of the elders at Ephesus St. Paul expressly says that "the Holy Ghost had made them overseers" over the Christian flock. So also when the first Apostolic Missionaries were sent forth, the personal direction of the Spirit is made as prominent as possible. "The Holy Ghost said, separate me Barnabas and Saul for the work unto which I have called them: so they, being sent forth by the Holy Ghost, departed unto Seleucia, and from thence unto Cyprus" So also when a solemn council is held to determine a momentous point of doctrine and practice, the decision is issued in this form, "it seemed good to the Holy Ghost and to us" And to complete this enumeration of what may be termed the larger and more commanding features of the case, we may pass to the preaching of St. Paul on his arrival in Rome. Just as the accusation brought against the High Priest and Council by Stephen, in his splendid apology for the faith, was "ye do always resist the Holy Ghost," so is St. Paul, at the end of the book, represented as saying to those who believed not: "Well spake the Holy Ghost by Esaias the prophet, saying, 'Hearing ye shall hear and shall not understand, and seeing ye shall see and not perceive.'" So do the Acts of the Apostles bear testimony to the Spirit "who spake by the prophets," bind together for us the Old Testament and the New, assure us of the fulfilment of the Saviour's promise, and introduce Christianity to the world as the dispensation of the Holy Ghost

And when we turn to the incidental allusions, if indeed we may correctly draw this distinction, we find them to be such as these The sin of Ananias and Sapphira is described as "a lie to the Holy Ghost," as an agreement "to tempt the Spirit of the Lord" The sin of Simon at Samaria was that he thought that the gift of the Holy Ghost might be "purchased with money." When Philip met the eunuch on the desert road near Gaza, it was the Spirit who said unto him, "go near;" and when this particular mission was ended, it was the Spirit who "caught him away, so that he was found at Azotus," and thence continued his mission through the cities to Cæsarea. When Ananias at Damascus was sent to Saul in his blindness, he declared that he was sent that Saul might be "filled with the Holy Ghost." When the churches throughout Judea and Galilee and Samaria "had rest," it is added with great beauty, that they were "edified and walking in the fear of the Lord and in the comfort of the Holy Ghost, were multiplied." When the prophet

Agabus in the early part of the history foretold famine, and when in the later part he foretold St Paul's imprisonment, in each case it is said that he did this "by the Spirit" When St Paul earnestly desired to preach the Gospel in a particular district, it is expressly said that he was "forbidden by the Holy Ghost," that the "Spirit suffered him not." When at Miletus he prophetically, though dimly, saw impending danger, his own language was: "I go bound in the Spirit to Jerusalem, not knowing the things that shall befall me there, save that the Holy Ghost witnesseth in every city, saying that bonds and afflictions abide me." Thus does the guidance, comfort, control, and discipline of the Holy Spirit appear at every point of the Acts of the Apostles, even as they are a present Divine power in every separate Christian life.

The supremacy of the Holy Ghost, this is the point to which I am always led upon a careful study of the Acts of the Apostles—the supremacy of the Holy Ghost in our system of doctrine and in the individual life.

This, too, is the inner meaning of the harmony of this book with the Gospels on the one hand and the Epistles on the other If there is one point above all others that I desire to express strongly at the close of the present course of lectures it is this.

And let me be permitted to say one word more regarding this culminating part of the teaching of the Acts of the Apostles, the supremacy of the Holy Ghost. It is by keeping this great doctrine in its prominent position that we keep all other religious truths in their right places. It is of the utmost moment that we should not only lay hold of the right elements of truth, but that we should apprehend them in their due relation and proportion to one another. It is through forgetfulness of this great principle, through distortion, through exaggeration in one place, through attenuating in another, rather than through positive error, that our Christianity ceases to be what it ought to be, that misunderstandings arise among us, that we become separated from each other. This great central book of the New Testament sets forth that great central truth which keeps all others in due subordination. The Acts of the Apostles, with their other blessings to the Church of Christ, come to us with the serious admonition that, fixing our eye on this cardinal point, "if we prophesy," we take heed to prophesy "according to the proportion of the faith."

Printed in Great Britain
by Amazon